THE GARDEN LOVER'S GUIDE TO

Spain

AND

Portugal

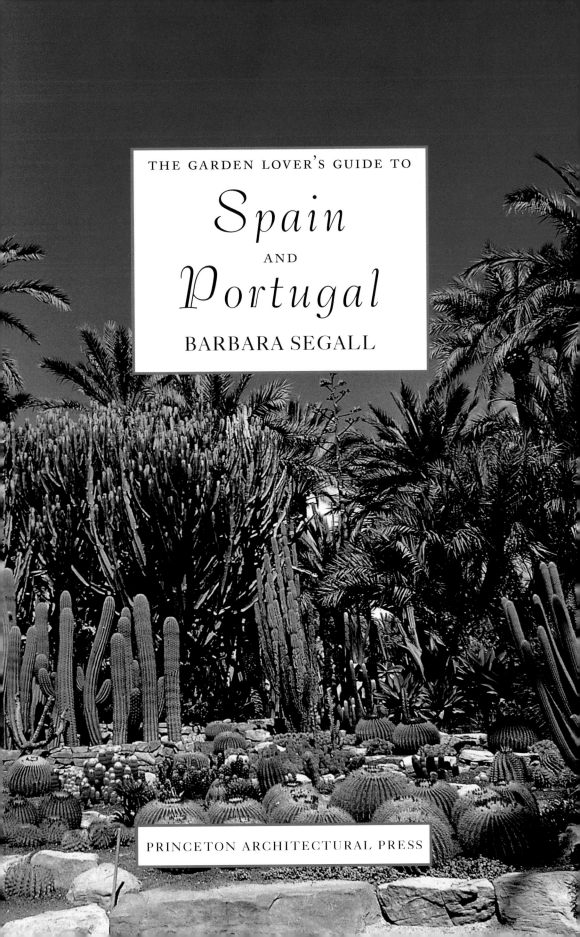

THE GARDEN LOVER'S GUIDE TO

Spain

AND

Portugal

BARBARA SEGALL

PRINCETON ARCHITECTURAL PRESS

First published in the United States in 1999 by
Princeton Architectural Press
37 East Seventh Street
New York, NY 10003
212.995.9620

For a catalog of other books published by Princeton Architectural Press,
call toll free 1.800.722.6657 or visit www.papress.com

First published in Great Britain in 1999 by Mitchell Beazley, an imprint of
Octopus Publishing Group Ltd, London

ISBN 1-56898-161-9

For Mitchell Beazley
Executive Art Editor: Vivienne Brar
Executive Editor: Alison Starling
Art Editor: Debbie Myatt
Designer: Terry Hirst
Editor: Selina Mumford
Production: Rachel Staveley
Picture Researcher: Jenny Faithfull
Illustrator: Kevin Robinson
Cartographer: Kevin Jones

For Princeton Architectural Press
Project Coordinator: Mark Lamster
Cover Design: Sara E. Stemen
Special thanks: Eugenia Bell, Jane Garvie, Caroline Green, Clare Jacobson,
Therese Kelly, and Annie Nitschke—Kevin C. Lippert, *publisher*

The publisher also expresses its thanks to all those who collated reference
material for the feature gardens.

All opening and closing hours are correct at the time of publication
but are subject to change. Readers are strongly advised to confirm hours
of operation before visiting the gardens included in this guide.

Half title page: Parc Samà
Title page: El Huerta del Cura
Contents page: Jardín Botánico Tropical "Pinya da Rosa"

Printed in China

Contents

How to use this book

This guide is intended for travellers who wish to visit the most historic and beautiful gardens of Spain and Portugal. The book is divided into five chapters covering the major regions. Each chapter comprises an introductory section with a regional map and a list of the gardens, followed by entries on each garden. The entries are accompanied by detailed at-a-glance information telling the reader about the garden's defining characteristics and nearby sights of interest. The guide also includes five "feature" gardens, specially illustrated by three-dimensional plans.

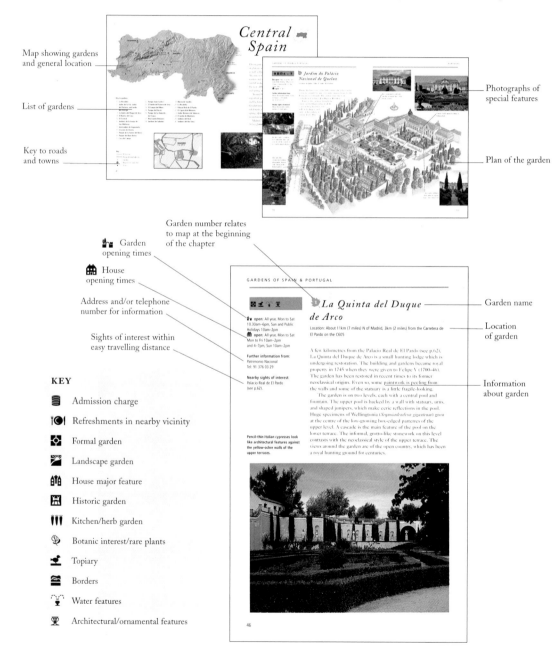

Map showing gardens and general location

List of gardens

Key to roads and towns

Photographs of special features

Plan of the garden

Garden number relates to map at the beginning of the chapter

Garden opening times

House opening times

Address and/or telephone number for information

Sights of interest within easy travelling distance

Garden name

Location of garden

Information about garden

KEY

🍳 Admission charge

🍴 Refreshments in nearby vicinity

✿ Formal garden

🌿 Landscape garden

🏛 House major feature

🏯 Historic garden

🌿 Kitchen/herb garden

🌸 Botanic interest/rare plants

🦆 Topiary

📚 Borders

⛲ Water features

🏺 Architectural/ornamental features

Preface

The late 20th-century tourist has more or less complete responsibility for putting Spain and Portugal "on the map" as prime holiday destinations. Many holiday-makers, however, are as unaware as their 18th-century counterparts, rich young men on the Grand Tour, were of "the real Spain and Portugal". Today, this includes the fast-growing tourism sector of garden visiting.

For the tourist taking shelter from sea, sun, and sand, there is more to Spain than "paseo and paella" and more to Portugal than "fado and bacalhao". For the garden visitor, these countries offer relatively untapped and unsophisticated, yet worthwhile sources of horticultural delight.

I found much to admire in grand and domestic gardens alike during my visits to over 150 gardens and landscapes in Spain and Portugal. The first rule for any visitor in a foreign country is to realize that the gardens are unlikely to be anything like those at home. Leave behind any preconceived ideas of what a garden is, and instead appreciate the gardens, parks, and historic sites for their own inimitable and individual characters.

A tiled pool complete with frogs in the Parque de María Luisa, Seville.

Introduction

The gardens of Spain and Portugal that are open to the public have their own distinct identities, but there are, however, some shared characteristics, most of them dating from the earliest recorded horticulture practised by the Muslim rulers of parts of both countries. Of these water for use and ornament holds the principal place. For the Moorish desert nomads, water was a life-giving element and was used for drinking, washing, cooling, cooking, and growing food for man and beast. It had ornamental qualities too. It made a pleasant sound when running, it was tranquil when still, and it reflected the sky and its surroundings.

In these early gardens, shelter or enclosure, and therefore privacy, was important. Today, there is still something private and separate about Spanish gardens. It is rare to be invited into the inner courtyard until you have forged a strong bond with your Spanish hosts. In Portugal there is a more relaxed, outward-looking feeling and garden visitors sense a more visible welcome.

Statuary and plants feature on every level of the Calvary staircase of Bom Jesus do Monte, near Braga.

Another common factor is the emphasis on trees and shrubs for foliage, shape, and flower, as well as for shade. Order, geometry, and regular patterning are also shared in many parts of Spain and Portugal. The palette of plants that early garden-maker's drew on accounts for other similarities. First, the Muslims brought many economic and ornamental plants into the region. During the 15th century when Spain and Portugal were founding their overseas empires, a vast range of plants was brought back by voyagers. Plants were a central component in an explorer's harvest: they could be the key to medicinal cures, to economic riches, as well as the means to satisfy hunger. In addition, their novelty and ornamental value ensured them a place on the estates and in the gardens of the wealthy.

In Spain the overriding influence on gardens, especially those in the south and north-eastern part of the country, derives from the Muslim conquest in the early 700s. Cordoba, Seville, and Granada are the centres where this influence carried on longest. And even in reconquered areas Muslim influence continued, known as Mudéjar (a hybrid of Muslim style) and carried out by Muslims for their new rulers. Later styles in Spanish gardens can be linked to a period of garden-making by successive monarchs. Under the Hapsburg Emperor, Carlos V, an Italianate Renaissance style made a brief but unsustained appearance in architecture and in gardens. During this period the Emperor abdicated and retired to the monastery at Yuste, where he awaited the end of his life close to the church and in sight of his garden.

His son, Felipe II, was more serious about gardens. On one occasion he wrote home to his daughter describing features he had seen in a Portuguese garden. His major

A pergola hung with a brightly coloured climbing plant at Sitio Litre, Tenerife.

Water moves slowly down the marble-faced stairway of Cascada Nueva at La Granja de San Ildefonso.

work was the palace and monastery of El Escorial (see p.47). He also developed the gardens at Aranjuez (see pp.44–5), where the clipped box hedges and compartmented parterrres were testimony to his Flemish upbringing and the influence of the Dutch gardeners who worked there.

Remnants of the original Parque del Buen Retiro in Madrid (see p.51), created for him by the Conde Duque de Olivares, still exist. Today, there are plans to restore the gardens to their original theatrical, rather Baroque, pleasure-garden status.

During the Bourbon period the most important garden created in Spain was at La Granja (see pp.48–9). It was the garden of Felipe V (1700–46) and was his nostalgic recreation of Versailles, the garden of his grandfather Louis XIV. La Granja has elements of the grandeur of Versailles, but without the unity and classicism of André Le Nôtre's designs for the former.

In the late 19th and early 20th centuries a number of public parks and garden projects were transformed at the hands of foreign and local landscape architects, including the French architect J C N Forestier, Antoni Gaudí, and Nicolau M Rubió i Tudurí.

Landscape design in the 20th century in Spain and Portugal is most visible in the garden landscapes created around new office complexes, residential projects, disused commercial sites, and tourist urbanizations, as well as in the golf courses and hotels that meet the needs of holiday-makers and visitors.

The plants that have been important in the gardens arrived in successive waves, brought by invaders and plant hunters. Today there is a new awareness of conservation and a desire to preserve and restore old gardens and to use indigenous plants, as well as the exotics that are so well adapted to their second homes in Spain and Portugal.

The great water tank and the Galeria dos Reis at Palácio Fronteira, Lisbon.

Key to gardens

1 Jardins de Costa i Llobera
2 Parc de la Ciutadella
3 Parc Güell
4 Parc del Laberint
5 Parc Laribal
6 Parc Joan Maragall
7 Jardins Miramar
8 Parc de Joan Miró
9 Jardins Mossèn Cinto Verdaguer
10 Jardins del Palau de Pedralbes
11 Monestir de Pedralbes
12 Jardins Vora el Mar
13 Jardí Cap Roig

14 Misión Botánica de Lourizán
15 Jardí Botànic Mar i Murtra
16 Pazo de Mariñán
17 Pazo de Oca
18 Monasterio de Piedra
19 Jardín Botánico Tropical "Pinya de Rosa"
20 Parque Quiñones de León
21 Parc Samà
22 Jardí de Santa Clotilde
23 Pazo de Santa Cruz de Rivadulla
24 Hostal de los Reyes Católicos

25 Pazo and Monasterio de San Lorenzo de Trasouto
26 La Finca Puente San Miguel
27 Parque Natural del Señorío de Bértiz
28 Pazo de Soutomaior

Also Jardí Botànic Barcelona (reopening before year 2000)

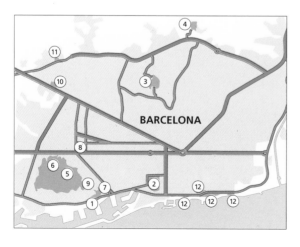

Key

=== Motorways
== Principal trunk highways
③ Gardens
● Major towns and cities
• Towns

12

Northern Spain

Spain's northern regions Galicia, Cantabria and Asturias, Old Castile and León, Aragón, the Basque provinces, and Navarra and Catalonia, from the west to the east coast, encompass a vast and changing landscape, as well as a range of climatic conditions. It is these differences that determine the individual characteristics of domestic life, and therefore gardens.

The west coast with its deeply indented coastline and tortuous winding roads down to the inlets, or *rías*, is known for its mild climate, the fertility of its soil, and the high rainfall it enjoys. In Galicia it is not unknown for annual rainfall to exceed 2m (6½ft). Frost does not occur in most parts of the region and the often humid conditions make for a verdant landscape. Galicia boasts some of Spain's oldest exotics, camellias. It is not unusual to see avenues of old camellias, such as those in the grounds of the former Pazo de Lourizán, now the Misión Botánica de Lourizán (see p.30). So important are these plants in Galician gardens that there is an annual Camellia Show, which rotates between Vigo, Pontevedra, and Vilagarcía.

A box parterre of great age fills the cloister gardens of the Monasterio de San Lorenzo de Trasouto.

A swamp cypress provides glowing colour at the lake edge in Parc Samà.

The softness of the climate permits many other imported ornamentals to thrive, and *Eucalyptus globulus*, *Magnolia grandiflora*, and *Cryptomeria japonica* of great age and massive size can be seen in many of the province's gardens, including Pazo de Oca (see p.32) and Pazo de Santa Cruz de Rivadulla (see p.36). At the latter there are other unlikely plants that owe their presence to the mild climatic conditions, such as an avenue of gnarled and ancient olives as well as the curious-looking Argentinean tree *Phytolacca dioica*.

Still in Galicia there are gardens where the natural exuberance of the vegetation has been well manicured into breathtaking parterres. In the small cloister garden of San Lorenzo de Trasouto (see p.37) the topiary is so lush and verdant that it seems more like a grassy sward, which you could walk across or even bounce up and down on, than a clipped parterre of shrubby plants.

On the sun-drenched shores of the Costa Brava, the rugged coast and climate have produced an opposite effect in gardens and in the range of plants used. Here tropical palms, fragrant shrubs, including *Pittosporum tobira*, and brightly coloured climbers, such as bougainvillea, are among the signature plants.

In this region an almost desert-like Mediterranean climate is the norm, with an average rainfall in January of 17–22mm (⅔–¾in). Night-time temperatures range from 9.5 to 13.5°C (49–56°F), while daytime temperatures soar to between 36 and 37.5°C (97–99°F). The natural vegetation of the coastal area is aromatic, scrubland inhabitants, all drought-loving, including broom, cistus, lavender, and thyme. Many of these plants have become the backbone of the gardens and landscapes of the region.

The city of Barcelona is well endowed with public parks and gardens of varying age and style:

Statuary and closely clipped box offer architectural shape at Parc del Laberint.

there are over 40 public landscapes listed by the city's Parks and Gardens Department. The oldest is the Parc de la Ciutadella (see p.17) designed by Josep Fontserè i Mestres. Within the park is a section designed by a French landscape architect J C N Forestier, whose name reappears throughout Spain in relation to landscapes as well as restorations in the early 1900s. He was responsible for landscaping Barcelona's Montjuïc Hill, above the port on the south of the city. There are several separate parks and gardens, including areas where his designs can still be seen in place. His was the plan for Barcelona's old Botanic Garden which closed in the 1990s. A site for a new botanic garden has been approved.

Another influential designer in the region was one of Forestier's pupils, Nicolau M Rubió i Tudurí. One of his creations is Jardí de Santa Clotilde (see p.35). Here pencil-straight Italian cypresses, hedges of perfumed *Pittosporum tobira*, and terraces softened with ivy-clad stairways make as much of an impact as the dramatic views out to sea that they gently disclose.

Views from the grounds of Soutomaior blend into the enclosing forest land.

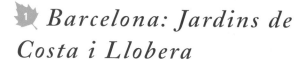

Barcelona: Jardins de Costa i Llobera

Location: Several entrances on the Carretera de Miramar, on the S side of Montjuïc

open: All year, daily, 10am; closes 9pm May to Aug, 8pm Apr and Sep, 7pm Mar and Oct, 6pm Nov to Feb

Further information from:
Institut Municipal de
Parcs i Jardins
Tel: 93 424 38 09

Nearby sights of interest:
Also on Montjuïc: Parc Joan Maragall (see p.25), Jardins Mossèn Cinto Verdaguer (see p.27), cable car, amusement park; Parc de Joan Miró (see p.26).

The massed flowers of *Cassia spectabilis* contrast with cacti on one of the lower terraces.

The view from this terraced garden is as dramatic as the collection of succulent plants and cacti that grow within its 6ha (15 acre) compass. Essentially a Mediterranean rock garden, it faces the sea and the busy, colourful commercial docks of Barcelona and seems to hang precipitously on the southern slope of Montjuïc. There are several entrances to the garden, at different levels. It is best to enter from the Carretera de Miramar and zig-zag across the garden to its viewpoint over the docks, where there is a large piece of statuary, in grey metal, towering over visitor and plants. It is the work of Josep Viladomat (1899–1989) and depicts a lacemaker.

Each terrace is filled with massed plantings and climbing plants, including bougainvillea. There are twelve species of palm trees, over 150 different cacti (mostly from the Americas), and over 200 species of succulents (from southern Africa). Other exotic trees include *Cassia spectabilis*, with its panicles of sunshine yellow flowers. Created at the end of the 1960s, the garden's south-east aspect allows for the cultivation of these tropical plants which are used to much warmer climates year-round.

The garden is full of colour and foliage interest throughout the year, with much winter display offered by the yellow, red, and orange flowers of aloes. In spring small bright mesembryanthemums from South Africa, in violet, orange, pink, and red, make a vibrant carpet of colour on the terraces. Cacti flower through the summer, followed in autumn, depending on species, by colourful fruits. The palms also flower and fruit in summer and autumn. All the while thick, silvery leaves of agaves and aloes, and the variety of prickles of the other succulents and cacti, provide a dramatic foliage display. The massed groupings of barrel cacti and the forests of upright cacti are compelling, even if you are not an enthusiast for this type of plant.

Barcelona: Parc de la Ciutadella

Location: NE of the old city, just S of the Olympic Village, with main entrances in Passeig Picasso, Passeig Pujades, and Carrer Wellington; parking is difficult, especially at weekends

open: All year, daily, 10am; closes 9pm May to Aug, 8pm Apr and Sep, 7pm Mar and Oct, 6pm Nov to Feb

Further information from:
Institut Municipal de
Parcs i Jardins
Tel: 93 424 38 09

Nearby sights of interest:
Parc Zoològic; Museu d'Art Modern; Parlament de Catalunya.

Although areas of this park are in need of restoration, it is full of life and activity and very popular with citizens and visitors of every age group. Built on the site of a former garrison, the creation of this park marks Barcelona's emergence from a military past into a civic role. It is the largest park in the city and covers an area of 31ha (76½ acres), 13 of which house the Zoo. It was designed by Josep Fontserè i Mestres and by 1888 was the setting of the International Exhibition, visited by some two million people. The main entrance, the impressive Arc de Triomf, was built for the Exhibition. Once in the park the formality of the two imposing right-angled avenues, one of horse chestnuts and lime trees and the other of white poplars, is apparent. Perfect for that Spanish pastime of strolling, the avenues give way to the romantic garden where evergreens, conifers, and palms, interspersed with deciduous trees, dominate.

The figure of Venus, backed by a scallop shell, dominates the cascade.

Of the many architectural features and statuary in the park, Antoni Gaudí's and Fontserè's imposing water feature is the most important. The Plaça d'Armes, roughly at the centre of the park, is a modern reworking in the early 1900s by the French landscape architect, J C N Forestier. Here Mediterranean plants including Aleppo pines, orange trees, oleanders, and cypresses are abundant. A circular lake with an island is popular, especially in mid-summer. Other buildings to visit include an *umbracle* or large wooden shadehouse and the former iron and glass greenhouse, now a cultural centre and café.

Barcelona: Parc Güell

Location: Main entrance on Carrer d'Olot, in the NW of Barcelona

open: All year, daily, 10am; closes 9pm May to Aug, 8pm Apr and Sep, 7pm Mar and Oct, 6pm Nov to Feb

open: Casa-Museu Gaudí: Mon to Fri 10am–2pm and 4–7pm, Sun 10am–2pm; admission charge

Further information from:
Institut Municipal de
Parcs i Jardins
Tel: 93 424 38 09

Nearby sights of interest:
Old residential quarter of Gràcia;
Parc de la Creueta del Coll.

Supported by huge pillars, the mosaic-encrusted roof is the base for a magnificent terrace.

Parc Güell, the best known of Barcelona's parks, offers on a large scale, 17ha (42 acres), a combination of architectural and landscape features with mature and natural-looking plantings. Intended to be a garden city of 60 building plots within a landscape park, Parc Güell was commissioned by Count Eusebi Güell in the 1890s. The project was abandoned in 1914, by which time its architect, Antoni Gaudí, had completed the famous features that are most enjoyed by the park's visitors today. Among them is the grand iron-balustraded entrance way, with its mosaic tilework on the walls, the imposing staircase dragon, the Hall of Columns supporting a mosaic portico ceiling (the area was intended as a market place for the garden city), the terrace above it, enclosed by the wonderfully curvaceous, never-ending bench covered in a mosaic of broken tiles, and the 3km (2 miles) of pathways. In 1922 the park became the property of Barcelona City Council and in 1984 UNESCO declared it a World Heritage site.

One of Gaudí's main intentions in the design of the park was that the natural beauty of the site, on the slopes of the Muntanya Pelada (the Treeless Mountain), should be emphasized by his structures. Gaudí used native plants in his planting and the result is a mature flora with carob, oak, and holm oak dominating.

There are several main entrances into the park. Not far from the tiles and dragons at one entrance, there is a choice of viaducts which lead up through the gardens by various stages. Most breathtaking of all is the view over Barcelona and the sea from the bench terrace. The continuous benches seem to swing out into the air, like an amusement-park ride, stopped in mid-flight and held in a time-frame. The open space of the terrace is often used for dancing the typical Catalan *sardana*.

Moving up from the terrace, the pathways lead through pergolas draped with bougainvillea, wisteria, and other climbing plants to the wilder and higher reaches of the park. Mature woodland plantings have blended with and softened what must once have been the dominating, stark and dramatic lines of the buildings and vaulting of paths and pavilions. Now the turrets and spires of the garden city buildings that were completed rise out of the vegetation and make their own ornamental statement.

To the left of the terrace is an area known as the Calvary, where Gaudí's paths and avenues have been interpreted as a pilgrim route towards salvation. This is situated at the highest point of the park with spectacular views over the city and the sea, and it affords a good perspective over the park itself. Some interpreters of Gaudí say that he was inspired by Montserrat, a monastery and place of pilgrimage outside Barcelona. The Calvary of the Three Crosses, as the rocky outcrop is known, stands out, apart from the lush vegetation.

The upper reaches of the park have been open to the public since 1984 and here there are groves of pines, olives, and plantings of *Acer negundo*, variegated and green privet, and the carob tree, *Ceratonia siliqua*. The mosaic tilework throughout the park is the work of one of Gaudí's contemporaries, the architect Josep M Jujol. The pathways are laid with ochre sand and make perfect surfaces for the play of light and shadow in the fierce heat of summer, absorbing the contrasting shapes of spiky palm tree fronds and more solid stems.

Although the visitor's response to the garden is usually expressed in terms of an appreciation of the architectural qualities of the buildings and hard landscape, there are examples of over 170 species grown here. Eucalyptus, acacia, olive, Japanese pittosporum (*Pittosporum tobira*), pistachio, and tamarisk are just a few plants that provide a variety of foliage and flower in various parts of the park.

Casa-Museu Gaudí, the home of Gaudí 1906–26, at the entrance of Parc Güell was built by Francesc Berenguer.

Palms and pots make a repetitive pattern at the rim of the upper terrace.

open: All year, daily, 10am to sunset; last entry is 1 hour before closing time; free entry Wed and Sun

Further information from:
Institut Municipal de
Parcs i Jardins
Tel: 93 424 38 09

Nearby sights of interest:
Parc de Collserola; amusement park on Mt Tibidabo.

The 14th-century turret dominates this Arabic-style house.

4 *Barcelona: Parc del Laberint*

Location: On the outskirts of Barcelona, 5km (3 miles) NW of the city centre

The Parc del Laberint, so-called because of the maze of smoothly clipped cypress hedges at its centre, is a superb example of a restored 18th-century neoclassical garden. The maze is the largest in Spain and consists of 750m (2,460ft) of Italian cypresses clipped into linear and curved shapes. Covering an area of 9ha (22 acres), the garden consists of many different zones including intricate water courses, woodland, and formal gardens. The garden was the creation of its 18th-century owner, the Marquis of Llupià and Alfarràs, Joan Desvalls, and his Italian architect,

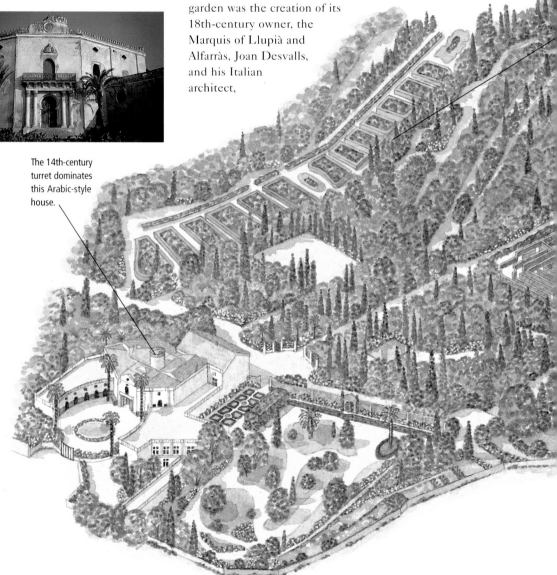

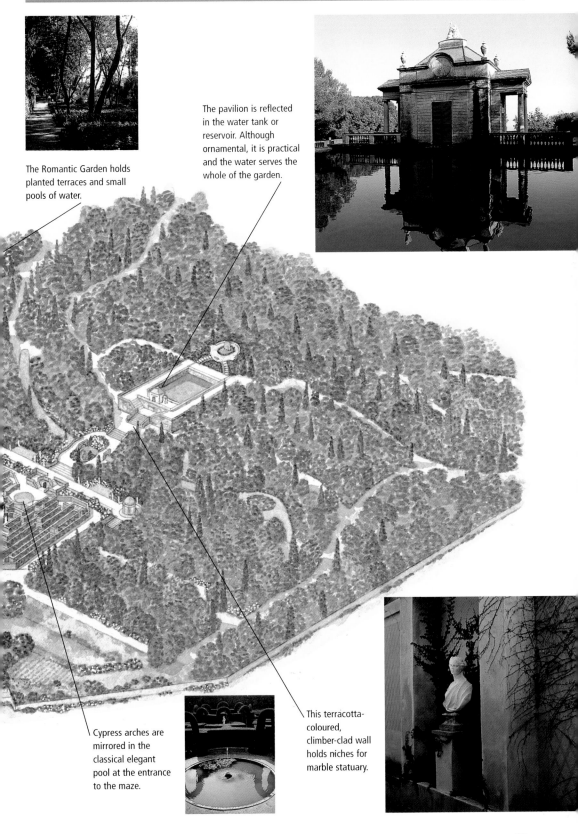

The Romantic Garden holds planted terraces and small pools of water.

The pavilion is reflected in the water tank or reservoir. Although ornamental, it is practical and the water serves the whole of the garden.

Cypress arches are mirrored in the classical elegant pool at the entrance to the maze.

This terracotta-coloured, climber-clad wall holds niches for marble statuary.

Domenico Bagutti. Work began in 1791 and was continued by descendants of the Marquis through several generations, with the garden used not only for the family's enjoyment but also as an open-air salon for social occasions and theatrical performances. In the late 19th century difficulties in maintaining the estate resulted in it passing into the ownership of the Barcelona municipal authorities. The garden had become run down, and some of the buildings and statuary were vandalized. After a programme of restoration it was reopened in the 1970s, but pressure of use and recurring vandalism once more damaged its fragile structure and in 1993 it was comprehensively restored, benefiting from EU subsidies. Now it is well maintained, and there is control on the number of people admitted during a given period.

Although you can wander at will through the garden, there is a well-planned and signed route which takes you around the house and into the Square of the Lions, where five paths meet. Here two marble lions, sitting high above the path atop the walls, commemorate the royal visit in 1827 of Fernando VII and his mother, María Luisa.

From one of the paths you can walk to the Box Garden, made up of geometric-shaped box hedges, at the side of the house. This leads to a small informal ornamental garden with camellias and a humorous piece of topiary in the shape of a table and chairs. From here you retrace your steps to the Square of the Lions and take one of the five paths direct to the maze of the Labyrinth. Statuary in this area includes Eros, the grotto of Echo and Narcissus, with bas-relief fountains, and a pair of pavilions

A statue of Eros stands at the centre of the maze of the Labyrinth.

22

housing statues of Danaë and Ariadne. You can take a path over a little bridge to cross the so-called Romantic Canal, built in 1853 by Elies Rogent and at one time navigable. The walk along the canal is attractive and there is an alternative route past the islet, known as "the Island of Love". The garden's paths lead upwards towards a pink, classical-style building decorated with friezes and blue shutters, the garden's main pavilion. The pavilion's back is reflected in the still waters of the square pool. Its ornamental qualities notwithstanding, the reservoir is vital for the water courses and irrigation of the park. Marking the end of the neo-classical part of the garden is a grotto complete with the reclining figure of a nymph, Egeria, and in front of it lie a fountain and pool, which are fed by one of three natural springs on the site.

Statuary and water spouts line the balustrade that encloses the large pond.

The main path now leads to an area of the garden with a distinctly romantic style, where fountains, waterfalls, and shady woodland vegetation dominate. Although not the original layout, this part of the garden has been recreated using the available documentation. The water and the path follow the course of an old gully and along its side are a series of flowerbeds and water features. Small pieces of sculpture resemble classical ruins and add to the sense of romanticism.

In spring the many flowering trees, including the Judas tree (*Cercis siliquastrum*), the ornamental orange (*Citrus aurantium* var. *amara*), tree of heaven (*Ailanthus altissima*), and the Japanese pittosporum (*Pittosporum tobira*), provide colour and fragrance. There are also some outstanding specimens of holm oak, Aleppo pine, and redwood in the park.

The nymph, Egeria, reclines in this ivy-clad grotto.

Barcelona: Parc Laribal

open: All year, daily, dawn to dusk

Location: On Montjuïc, accessible at several entry points from the roads that border it including Avinguda Estadi and Miramar, and Passeig de Santa Madrona

Further information from:
Institut Municipal de
Parcs i Jardins
Tel: 93 424 38 09

Nearby sights of interest:
Parc de Joan Miró (see p.26);
Museu Arqueològic; amusement
park on Mt Tibidabo.

Although one of Barcelona's historic gardens, Parc Laribal is a shadow of its former self. It was created between 1916 and 1918 by J C N Forestier. His design for a Mediterranean-style terraced garden using strong architectural forms, such as pergolas, water canals, and fountains, linked elements of the Hispano-Arab past to the present, and marked a turning point in Catalan style. Huge wooden pergolas, supported on tall brick piers or white stone columns, clothed with climbing plants that cascaded with flowers in summer, helped to create a hanging garden. Much of the architectural structure such as stairs, paths, pergolas, and water features remains. Many of the trees, including huge plane trees, *Erythrina falcata*, *Lagunaria patersonii*, and *Tipuana tipo*, are from Forestier's original planting, but the flowerbeds have been replaced by groupings of aromatic herbs. Other plants that thrive include *Pittosporum tobira* and *Quercus ilex*, shaped into mophead forms, and everywhere, ivy clothes the ground.

Dense plantings of lavender, rosemary, and other aromatic herbs have replaced the original flowerbeds.

A fairly busy road runs by the garden and parts of it have more or less become unofficial play areas for children from a nearby school. All this diminishes the garden's original character. Nevertheless, a visit to this garden provokes an eerie, almost ghostly, sense of its past glory.

Barcelona: Parc Joan Maragall

Location: The grounds of the Palauet Albéniz; entrance gates at point where Esplanada del Palau Nacional de Montjuïc and Avinguda Estadi meet, on Montjuïc

The gardens form the grounds around the Palauet Albéniz, built to welcome King Alfonso XIII on his visit in 1929 to the International Exhibition. In 1970 the mansion became the official residence for the Spanish royal family in Barcelona. The property is sometimes occupied by other visiting dignitaries, and it is for this reason that the public are admitted only for a short period each week. Opened in 1970 the 3.6ha (8¾ acre) garden was designed by Joaquim M Casamor in a French classical style.

Close to the mansion formal parterres, planted with colourful bedding, are endowed with a pair of classical-style fountains. Much of the grounds are laid to sweeping lawns, with large specimen trees, statuary, and several water features, including a lake with weeping willows. An attractive, gently moving stairway of water makes a strong feature near one of the property's gates. There is also an open-air theatre here.

open: All year, Sun, 10am–2pm

Further information from:
Institut Municipal de Parcs i Jardins
Tel: 93 424 38 09

Nearby sights of interest:
1992 Estadi Olímpic;
Museu Etnòlogic.

A water staircase leads to a pool with statuary on its edge.

Barcelona: Jardins Miramar

Location: On Montjuïc, mid-way up the S side and accessible from Avinguda Miramar, Passeig Miramar, and Passeig Josep Carner

Resplendent with bedding plants and clipped cypresses, Jardins Miramar offer striking views over the Mediterranean coastline and the city of Barcelona, especially the Gothic Quarter and the Eixample. Not quite at the seaside, but certainly of it, the gardens are formal, symmetrical, and make a bright display all through the summer months. The gardens are arranged on terraces in full sun, making them ideal for strolling.

open: All year, daily, dawn to dusk

Further information from:
Institut Municipal de Parcs i Jardins
Tel: 93 424 38 09

Nearby sights of interest:
Places on Montjuïc: Jardins Mossèn Cinto Verdaguer (see p.27); Parc Joan Maragall (see above); cable car; amusement park.

8 *Barcelona: Parc de Joan Miró*

Location: In the city centre a few blocks W of the Plaça de Espanya; there are entrances on all four streets that enclose the park, including Carrer Tarragona

open: All year, daily, 10am; closes 9pm May to Aug, 8pm Apr and Sep, 7pm Mar and Oct, 6pm Nov to Feb

Further information from:
Institut Municipal de
Parcs i Jardins
Tel: 93 424 38 09

Nearby sights of interest:
Poble Espanyol (a Spanish village built for the International Exhibition of 1929); Plaça de Espanya; Mies van der Rohe Pavelló.

Dona i Ocell by Joan Miró dominates the modern park built on the site of an old slaughter house.

Built on the site of an old slaughter house, the park's 4.7ha (11½ acres) fill a city block in a roughly rectangular shape. Designed by a group of Barcelona landscape architects, including Beth Galí, the park has two parts. One, a bare concrete base with a pool, is the sparse setting for a 22m (72ft) high sculpture by Catalan artist Joan Miró. Officially entitled *Dona i Ocell* (Woman and Bird), it towers high above the pool and park and it is easy to see why it is still known locally by its original name "The Cock"!

From this empty, barren space you can see the tree tops and greenery that make up the rest of the park. Here the geometric shapes made by wide paths are enforced by the ranks of statuesque palms, planted in long lines. In contrast to the open space around the sculpture this area is luxuriant, rather like an oasis. All the paths, and even the play areas, are covered with a yellow-ochre coloured, sandy surface.

The palm trees provide strong architectural features, as well as welcome shade in summer. The tall stone pergola piers, which echo the straight trunks of the palms as they support massive beams, are hung with colourful climbing plants. One of the entrances to the park is through an imaginative gate by Galí. In iron, it portrays larger-than-life-size children to bar the way when shut and when open the "children of the gate" lead the way to a library, also housed in the park.

The overall design of the park is unfussy and the plantings rely for their effect on a small range of plants, grouped in a dramatically large scale. The shadows of palms and pergolas make their own play of light and shade on the yellow surfaces. Not quite biblical, but certainly evocative of North African and Arabic landscapes, this park which opened in 1986 is used for strolling, sitting, and playing.

9 *Barcelona: Jardins Mossèn Cinto Verdaguer*

Location: On Montjuïc, just below the castle of Montjuïc, off Avinguda Estadi

open: All year, daily, 10am; closes 9pm May to Aug, 8pm Apr and Sep, 7pm Mar and Oct, 6pm Nov to Feb

This green and shady garden is situated on a steep slope on the side of a former stone quarry. The garden is at its best in spring when over 100,000 bulbous plants including narcissi, tulips, hyacinths, and fritillaria bloom. It is, in fact, a garden dedicated to bulbous and rhizomatous plants, so spring colour is followed by daylilies, iris, and dahlias. Created in 1970, its grassy gradients are well planted with trees, including cluster pines and columnar cypresses, which offer welcome shade in summer and ensure an attractive year-round green backdrop for the colourful flowers.

Water plays an important role in this garden and the main feature is an attractively landscaped series of paths and benches, with rectangular ponds that descend from a reservoir at the top of the garden. The ponds are full and the impression is that they overflow into each other, but, in fact, they don't. The overall effect is of a descending staircase of water. Water plants thrive here and marginal plants and grasses grow at their side and overhang benches on each level. At the lowest level of the garden is a circular pool, with mature trees around it including a good specimen of the swamp cypress, *Taxodium distichum*.

The garden is named after the poet Cinto Verdaguer, one of the most important Catalan literary figures, who widened the scope and influence of the Catalan language, taking it from a domestic level into a wider, more public arena.

Further information from:
Institut Municipal de
Parcs i Jardins
Tel: 93 424 38 09

Nearby sights of interest:
Parc Joan Maragall (see p.25); 1992 Estadi Olímpic; Museu Arqueològic; Poble Espanyol (a Spanish village built for the International Exhibition 1929).

Peaceful pools holding aquatic plants alternate with stone seats.

10 *Barcelona: Jardins del Palau de Pedralbes*

Location: On the Avinguda Diagonal, towards the W of Barcelona, opposite the Palau-Reial underground station

open: All year, daily, 10am; closes 9pm May to Aug, 8pm Apr and Sep, 7pm Mar and Oct, 6pm Nov to Feb

In 1919 the Can Feliu and land owned by Count Eusebi Güell (of Güell Park) was offered as an official residence in Barcelona for the royal family. In the 1920s the newly acquired land was amalgamated with the existing estate and the result was the creation of a garden designed by Nicolau M Rubió i Tudurí. In 1960 the palace and the gardens were opened to the public.

Such was Rubió's skill that he created a classical garden in what he described as a "geometric decorative" style, yet incorporated many of the original plantings of the former estates including an

Further information from:
Institut Municipal de
Parcs i Jardins
Tel: 93 424 38 09

Nearby sights of interest:
Palau de Pedralbes and Museu de Ceràmica; Monestir de Pedralbes (see p.28).

avenue of limes, many cedars, and pines. Ivy, as a ground cover on a grand scale planted under trees and lining deep beds, gives the shade a shining glow.

There are many wide and leafy avenues with classical urns set at focal points where path axes cross, and statuary which seems to grow out of sweeping lawns or glassy pools. There is colour from flowering trees, climbers, and bulbous plants, but the overall impression is of a serene and leafy haven. Behind the palace itself, the gates and gatehouses to the original Güell lands, made of iron by Antoni Gaudí, are worth seeking out, as is the shady, plant-covered arbour he created out of an iron canopy.

open: All year, Tue to Sun, 10am–2pm; admission charge is reduced Wed (if not a holiday) and free entry first Sun of month
open: All year, Tue to Sat 10am–5pm, Sun 10am–2pm; free entry first Sun of month

Further information from:
Pedralbes Monastery Museum,
Baixada del Monestir, 9,
08034 Barcelona
Tel: 93 203 92 82/91 16

Nearby sights of interest:
Collecció Thyssen-Bornemisza of art is housed in the monastery (separate admission charge; open Tue to Fri and Sun 10am–2pm, Sat 10am–5pm).

The cloister garden holds palms and fruit trees, as well as herbs.

11 *Barcelona: Monestir de Pedralbes*

Location: At the western end of the Avinguda Pedralbes, which runs off the Avinguda Diagonal 5km (3 miles) NW of the city centre

The monastery was founded in 1326 by Queen Elisenda for the Franciscan order of nuns, the Poor Clares. In 1983 the Poor Clares moved to a nearby building and the monastery, including its wonderfully preserved and (up until then) continuously used three-storeyed cloister, was opened to the public. The fact that the monastery was so recently in use as a working community, coupled with the sensitive preservation of the cells, infirmary, and communal rooms, makes it possible to imagine the life of the order going on around you. This is especially so in the magnificent Gothic cloister. Each side has 26 columns, making it one of the largest in the world.

The cloister garden was redesigned using all the available written records. Oranges, lemons, roses, and jasmine were among the plants used. Tall cypresses, palms, citrus, and loquats offer shade, fragrance, and fruits, and the small herb garden is filled with aromatic herbs such as lavender and rosemary. It is sited just opposite the pharmacy, which was used by the nuns until the 1940s. At the opposite end of the cloister is a 14th-century cistern. The tiled benches mark its outer edges and water was taken up from a well and spring for drinking, washing, and watering the cloister gardens.

From the 16th-century infirmary the view out of the windows is onto the Hort Petit or small garden. This and the Hort Gran, or big garden, are still cultivated by the nuns but neither is visitable.

12 *Barcelona: Jardins Vora el Mar (Parks by the Sea)*

Location: On the seafront adjacent to the Vila Olímpica

Jardins Vora el Mar is the collective name for six modern parks created along the seafront at Sant Martí de Provençals. They were completed in time for the 1992 Barcelona Olympics and cover an area of almost 30ha (74 acres). Parc de Carles I is near the main entrance to the Olympic Village and is bounded on one side by a busy motorway. It is protected from this by grassy mounds and ranges of pines and cypresses. Parallel to the seafront are Parc de les Cascades, Parc del Port, Parc d'Icària, and Parc del Poble Nou.

Fountains are an important feature of the aptly named Parc de les Cascades, which is planted with Mediterranean plants. The Parc del Port, which sweeps right down to the sea, is full of oranges, carob, and typically Mediterranean aromatic shrubs and trees, such as Jerusalem sage, lavender, laurels, and pines.

The parks are imaginative and hold large pieces of specially created statuary, as well as items borrowed from the area's mixed industrial and maritime past, including hulls of ships which emerge from the landscape.

open: At all times

Further information from:
Institut Municipal de
Parcs i Jardins
Tel: 93 424 38 09

Nearby sights of interest:
Parc de la Ciutadella (see p.17);
Vila Olímpica; the beaches: Platja
Nova Icària, Platja Bogatell, Platja
Mar Bella, Platja Nova Mar Bella.

The central pool in Parc d'Icària.

---

13 *Jardí Cap Roig*

Location: 1km (¾ mile) S of Calella de Palafrugell, 45km (28 miles) SE of Girona via the N255

The garden at Cap Roig began in 1924 when the property was bought by Colonel and Madame de Woevodsky. Together they created a garden on what was a bare and precipitous headland of the Costa Brava, turning it, over a number of years, into a paradise for typical Mediterranean plants, as well as for cacti and succulents. Their first project was to plant the 40ha (99 acre) site with pines to achieve shade and cover.

The garden is laid out on oblong terraces descending the slope, with fountains and pools on different levels. Each terrace is enclosed within high hedges which hold the fragrance of plants during the heat of the day, as well as in the cool of the evening. In 1971 they gave their land and home to the Spanish government. It is still open to the public and although brightly planted, it lacks the creativity of its originators. From viewpoints there are breathtaking views to the sea and along the coast.

open: Daily, summer
9am–9pm, winter 9am–6pm

Further information from:
Caixa de Girona, Department
d'Obra Social, Apartat Correos
no 58, 17080 Girona

Nearby sights of interest:
Fishing village of Roses; old
quarter of Cadaqués, a fishing
village now a centre for artists
and writers; port of Calella de
Palafrugell; views from the
corniche road between Sant Feliu
de Guíxols and Tossa de Mar.

Misión Botánica de Lourizán

open: All year, daily, dawn to dusk; guided tour by appointment only

Further information from:
Centro de Investigaciones Forestales
Lourizán, 36080 Pontevedra
Tel: 986 85 64 00
Fax: 986 85 64 20

Nearby sights of interest:
Pontevedra, a traditional Galician town; Ría de Pontevedra; the village of Combarro, on the north shore, is famous for its collection of *hórreos* (granaries) on the waterfront; Vigo, Spain's principal transatlantic port where the old fishing quarter is particularly attractive.

A typical granary or *hórreo* in the grounds of the former Pazo de Lourizán.

Location: S of Pontevedra on the A9 in the direction of Marín, but turning off to Lourizán before getting to Marín

Situated on an elevated position above the Ría de Pontevedra, the estate and garden of the former Pazo de Lourizán are still of interest for the collection of camellias and tree ferns, and the arboretum. However, the site now houses the headquarters of the Centro de Investigaciones Forestales Lourizán whose funding for maintaining the grounds is often under pressure. In addition, the garden and the surrounding area can be blighted by the smell and sight of smoke from the paper factory, just outside Pontevedra. That said, the bones of the garden that once belonged to Eugenio Montero Ríos, an influential politician and lawyer, are still visible and offer a poignant reminder of the temporary nature of man-made landscapes.

Of particular note is the use of *Ophiopogon jaburan*, which was introduced into Europe in 1784 and used at Lourizán since the 1930s as a ground cover in dense shade. One of the most striking

remnants of the past is an avenue of camellias, some 7.5m (25ft) high, that arches over and meets, completely shading one of the former carriageways. A damp and mossy grotto, a round pigeon loft, and a ruined pumping station are among the architectural features. A huge slab of granite is still in place as a picnic table. Shaded by a wisteria-clad iron pergola it evokes the outdoor life once enjoyed here, while a "running" vine-covered pergola leads you up a hill. A small stream twists by its side.

The staff at the Research Centre are involved in carrying out trials on North American and other conifers. Other trials include analysis of disease-resistance in Spanish chestnuts. Eucalyptus, such as *Eucalyptus grandis* and *E. globulus*, are also on trial for economic uses. Another Australasian plant, a conifer, *Dascridium cupresinum*, with its trailing branches, is being trialled for its possible use in floristry.

Jardí Botànic Mar i Murtra

Location: Blanes, Costa Brava; parking is limited, but the garden can be reached after a steep, winding climb or on a local bus from Blanes

 open: Daily, Apr to Oct 9am–6pm, Nov to Mar 10am–5pm

Further information from:
Jardí Botànic Mar i Murtra, Passeig Karl Faust 10, 17300 Blanes, Girona
Tel: 972 33 08 26

Nearby sights of interest:
Beach resorts on Costa Brava.

The garden was begun in 1921 by German businessman Karl Faust (1874–1952). Covering 16.5ha (41 acres), it was intended as a scientific site preserving the indigenous character of the coastal Mediterranean flora. Today, the garden is maintained by the Karl Faust Foundation and about one-third of the property is open to the public.

Faust created several different gardens to house the plants that he collected from all over the world. Mar i Murtra is now divided into tropical, temperate, and Mediterranean garden areas and houses some 3,500 species, including bamboos, cacti, conifers, palms, and succulents. Well-signed paths lead you through plantings from African and American arid zones, on to huge clumps of well-established bamboos in the temperate garden, and then down the slope towards the shimmering blue sea, where indigenous Mediterranean plants thrive, as well as those from Australia, South Africa, and Chile.

All routes down the hill lead to a classical-style temple named in honour of Linnaeus, from where it is pleasant to contemplate the sea and the myrtles which, in Catalan, form the name of this garden. Although it has the word botanic in its title, it is not in any way a botanic garden such as that of Madrid (see pp.56–9).

Typical Canary Island plants, such as the dragon-tree, are grown on this terrace near the entrance.

Pazo de Mariñán

Location: On the Ría de Betanzos, on the Galician coast, 4km (2½ miles) N of Betanzos on the LC163

 open: By appointment, during the week only and not on Public Holidays

Further information from:
Relaciones públicas, Diputación provincial de La Coruña, Alferez Provisional, 15006 La Coruña
Tel: 981 18 33 21

Nearby sights of interest:
Coastal town of Sada, with a turn-of-the-century boardwalk and views across the *ría* (inlet); Betanzos, town with attractive town square.

Although no longer inhabited by an individual family the formal gardens and grounds at Mariñán are well maintained. The house has been painted white, but the typical grey granite stone of the double staircase that leads down to a box-edged parterre still makes a dramatic impact. Intricate patterning made by the neatly clipped box ribbons in the parterre is at odds with the palms that tower high above the garden. Myrtles and thuja have escaped from the shapes they were probably once clipped to, and sprawl out of the box boundaries. The grounds of the *pazo* go down to the edge of the sea inlet, where the property is enclosed within a stone wall. A woodland area with mature specimens of pines and conifers also includes some of the oldest *Eucalyptus globulus* in Galicia. Winter and spring are the best times for enjoying the camellias in the informal gardens between woodland and parterre.

🏰 **open:** Summer, daily,
9am–1pm and 4–8pm; free
entry Mon am

Further information from:
Tourist Office, Villar 43, 15705
Santiago de Compostela,
La Coruña
Tel: 981 58 40 81

Nearby sights of interest:
Pazo de Santa Cruz de Rivadulla
(see p.36); Santiago de Compostela,
old city is a focus for pilgrims.

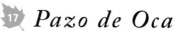

17 *Pazo de Oca*

Location: In San Esteban de Oca, near Valboa, some 25km (15½ miles) SE of
Santiago de Compostela, off the N525

Silvery-grey Galician granite is the material used for the main
architectural features at Pazo de Oca. Used for walls, water
courses, fountains, steps, and balustrades for the large pools and,
indeed, for the fabric of the 18th-century manor house itself, it
makes a strong framework for the plantings. The entrance to the
garden is through an arched doorway which leads into a world
of giant, mature specimens of *Camellia reticulata, Cryptomeria
japonica*, and *Magnolia grandiflora*.

Water plays an important part in the garden's function, as
well as in its ornament. In the property's early history there was a
mill near the large stone reservoir at the highest point of the garden.
From here the stream that fed it begins its course through stone
channels and fountain spouts to the large, still pool which makes
the most memorable impression. The pool, encircled by a
box-lined path, lies at the secret heart of the garden. It is made
even more secret by the box, which towers several metres above
the path. The pool itself is boat-shaped and its edge is marked
with pyramidal and round finials of stone. But the most delightful
element, at the centre of the pool, is a wonderful piece of
statuary: a stone boat, filled with hydrangeas, with two rather
courtly mariners or fishermen standing fore and aft.

A grape-clad pergola follows a path through some plantings
of fruit trees, towards a private kitchen garden, and there is a
recently planted small maze of lavender on the route back to the
entrance courtyard.

This stone boat, built in the
mid-18th century, holds a mass
of hydrangeas.

Monasterio de Piedra

Location: Near the village of Nuévalos, 11km (7 miles) SE of Alhama de Aragón

The remains of a former 12th-century Cistercian monastery built here have been converted into a hotel, and there are guided tours of the cloister, chapter house, kitchen, refectory, cellars, and abbey church. The grounds of the monastery were landscaped in the 1860s by Juan Federico Muntadas, an exponent of the romantic movement. He created a wild and natural-looking park using the River Piedra as the main focus for his creation. Lakes, grottoes, waterfalls, cascades, and caves are all part of his design. The trail through the park takes about three hours to complete.

One of the most dramatic miradors overlooks a waterfall called the Horse's Tail. The route leads up to the Devil's Cliff and down to the Mirror Lake. Before Muntadas worked his transformation, the site was covered in forest. In the wooded areas that remain there are good stands of ash and elder, as well as *Celtis australis*.

open: All year, daily, 9am until dusk

Further information from:
Monasterio de Piedra, 50210 Nuévalos, Zaragoza
Tel: 976 84 90 11
Fax: 976 84 90 54

Nearby sights of interests:
City of Zaragoza; Alhama de Aragón; Daroca, attractive medieval town with battlements.

Jardín Botánico Tropical "Pinya de Rosa"

Location: Near Santa Cristina, between Blanes and Lloret de Mar on the Costa Brava

"Pinya de Rosa" was developed by the late Fernando Riviere de Caralt, a civil engineer and succulent specialist, who bought the property in 1945. It is arranged in terraced sections that follow the contours of the site. Stone walls and gravel paths intensify the heat in summer and the collections of succulents and cacti, together with palms, add to the exotic, sun-baked atmosphere. Over 7,000 species are represented, arranged systematically in the various areas. The collection of opuntia, containing 600 species in 18 genera, is regarded as the most important in the world. There are also good selections of lithops, aloe, mesembryanthemum, agave, and yucca. Whether the collections are in flower or not, and there is a long season starting with aloes in winter, the structure of the modified leaves and stems of these plants offer an equally dramatic beauty throughout the year. The number of plants are increased year on year with some 1,500 species sown.

open: Daily, summer 9am–6pm, winter 10am–4pm

Further information from:
Jardín Botánico Tropical "Pinya de Rosa", Blanes, Costa Brava

Nearby sights of interest:
Jardí Botànic Mar i Murtra (see p.31); Museu Municipal, Tossa de Mar (Chagall's *The Flying Violinist*).

Barrel cactus (*Echinocactus grusonii*) seem to jostle, prickle to prickle, in a colony.

20 *Parque Quiñones de León*

Location: 2km (1¼ miles) SW of Vigo on the C550

open: All year, daily,
9am–9pm

open: Museo Municipal: 1 Oct
to 30 Apr, Tue to Sat 9am–7pm,
Sat and festivals 10am–2pm;
1 May to 30 Sep, Tue to Sat
9am–8pm, Sun and festivals
10am–2pm

Further information from:
Museo Municipal Quiñones de
León, Parque de Castrelos,
36213 Vigo
Tel: 986 29 50 70

Palms rise above a box parterre.

Parque Quiñones de León dates from the last decades of the
19th century and was laid out by a firm from Oporto, Portugal. It
consists of several different garden areas and the main attractions
are the neatly maintained formal gardens in the front of the house,
the parterre, the rose garden, and the romantic landscaped garden
with mature magnolias and planes.

At the back of the *pazo*, the so-called "French" or parterre
garden, framed by closely clipped box hedges, with its symmetrical
design and simplicity of composition, makes a strong architectural
statement. Nearby are several specimens of *Camellia japonica*,
including one that is said to be the oldest in Europe as well as
the biggest in Galicia.

Palms, a tulip tree, and magnolias, as well as oak, yew, and
other conifers, are among the specimen trees in the geometric
layout that leads off from the parterre. On a higher level than
the parterre is a terraced rose garden, with paths and walls lined
with roses. Rambling roses arch and wave their blooms along a
walkway set with stone heraldic shields.

A section of the park, described as the "English" garden, has
a more natural woodland look, with large planes and magnolias
making dense cover. The garden is waymarked and there are
information panels about the plants and birds it holds.

---

21 *Parc Samà*

Location: Between Cambrils and Montbrió, off motorway E15 at exit 37,
17km (10½ miles) W of Tarragona

open: All year, daily,
9am–6pm; closes Public Holidays

Further information from:
Parc Samà, 43391 Vinyols,
Tarragona
Tel: 977 82 60 05

Nearby sights of interest:
Tarragona: the cathedral
(13th-century cloister with
garden full of orange trees)
and Roman ruins.

Romantic in style, Parc Samà was founded by Salvador Samà
Torrens (1861–1933), Marquis of Marianao, and work began on the
garden in 1881. He lived with his family in Cuba and much of the
property is in a colonial style. He commissioned Josep Fontserè
i Mestres to design the garden. The exotic tower is thought to
be the work of Antoni Gaudí, working under Fontserè's guidance.

Although some of the plantings are relaxed and informal
much of it has a plantation style, with, for example, mandarins
arranged geometrically. In front of the house are several
100-year-old specimens of lime, chestnut, and *Quercus robur*.
The park is renowned for its good collection of palms, including
Phoenix canariensis, Chamaerops excelsa, C. humilis, and *Washingtonia
filifera*, and the exotic atmosphere is heightened by items such as
a large, richly coloured enamelled vase brought to the garden in

1881 from Vichy, France. In the wooded area at the back of the house are fine specimens of *Pinus pinea*, *P. halepensis*, and *Cedrus deodara*. Three islands lie on the lake and on the largest of these is a mountain made of large stones, complete with a grotto. Bridges to the island are balustraded with rustic-looking sides, but they are in fact made of cement. Of great beauty is the *Taxodium distichum*, which grows on the lake edge and has the most dramatic leaf colour in autumn.

 # *Jardí de Santa Clotilde*

Location: S of Lloret de Mar on the Costa Brava

Santa Clotilde is a large property set on a rocky hillside on the Costa Brava. Built on the site of an old vineyard, the garden has a timeless, dreamlike quality. Begun in the 1920s by the late Marquis of Roviralta, it has reached a breathtaking maturity with elegant cypresses towering above the neatly clipped hedges of *Pittosporum tobira*. In the creation of the garden the Marquis had the services of Nicolau M Rubió i Tudurí, then a young landscape architect, who was just beginning to make his mark. Together they executed an Italianate garden in the Renaissance style, where symmetry of paths, planting, and focal points define the garden.

Stately Italian cypresses, Monterey cypress, and stone pines, as well as the hedges, hide the sea from full view, allowing only tantalizing glimpses of silvery-blue, and it is only at focal points or at specially created viewpoints that you come out into the open and see the water shimmering ahead. You can wander through this garden in any direction, but the tendency of the site impels you either downwards, on magnificent stairways flanked with statuary, or along the wide, impeccably raked gravel terraces.

One of the most attractive features of the stairs, softening and blending them with the overall greenery of the garden, are the risers, where glossy-leaved ivy has been trained across from side to side. In all seasons the evergreen foliage of pittosporum, pines, oleander, and viburnum makes the strongest impact, but in summer colour from the flowers of agapanthus, oleander, hydrangeas, roses, and clivia compete with fragrance of the Japanese pittosporum and the aromatic pine needles.

open: By appointment

Further information from:
Head Gardener, Jardí de Santa Clotilde, Avinguda Sta Clotilde, Lloret de Mar, Girona
Tel: 972 36 21 53

Nearby sights of interest:
Seaside town of Blanes; Jardí Botànic Mar i Murtra (see p.31); Jardí Cap Roig (see p.29); Jardín Botánico Tropical "Pinya de Rosa" (see p.33).

Ivy-clad risers make the whole stairway a shimmering green.

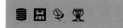

open: By appointment

Further information from:
Marqués de Santa Cruz de Rivadulla, Santa Cruz de Rivadulla, La Coruña
For appointment, contact nursery:
Ortigueira SA, 15880 Santa Cruz de Rivadulla, La Coruña
Tel: 981 51 20 11

Nearby sights of interest:
Pazo de Oca (see p.32); Santiago de Compostela; towns and villages on the bays and inlets of the coast.

A leafy canopy overhangs one of several ponds.

23 *Pazo de Santa Cruz de Rivadulla*

Location: In Rivadulla, 18km (11¾ miles) SE of Santiago de Compostela off the N525, by Km 323

This lush and romantic garden is spread out over 2ha (5 acres). It has been the property of the family of the present Marquis of Santa Cruz de Rivadulla since 1520 and the estate as a whole has supported agriculture in the shape of flax, wheat, and sugarcane, and later corn and potatoes. In the 20th century it runs a dairy herd and produces fruit, wine, and a mouth-tingling *eau-de-vie*.

Each generation of the family has brought plants of interest to the garden, which reflect the introductions of the period. A *Magnolia grandiflora* of great size and age, as well as the curious-looking ombu tree, *Phytolacca dioica*, with its grotesque trunk and root structure are among the specimens to marvel at.

The tour of the garden, usually guided by the gardener, takes you away from the house towards several water features. The way is punctuated by stops to admire plantings of camellias, as well as a tunnel formed by the overhanging branches of box trees grown to over 4m (13ft). Stone steps and rustic paths lead down to an old grist mill, several large ponds, and then to the man-made cascade. A circular pool is surrounded by the umbrella-like leaves of *Gunnera manicata*. Two 30m (98ft) high thread palms make their way heavenward, side-by-side, at the pool's edge.

The family have, over generations, specialized in collecting camellias and the majority of plants sold at their Ortigueira Nursery are camellia cultivars raised on the property.

open: All year, daily, as it is a *parador* (hotel) and there is no charge to guests

Further information from:
Parador de Santiago de Compostela, Praza do Obradoiro 1, 15705 Santiago de Compostela, La Coruña
Tel: 981 58 22 00
Fax: 981 56 30 94

Nearby sights of interest:
Cathedral; Pazo de Raxoi (town hall); old city.

24 *Santiago de Compostela: Hostal de los Reyes Católicos*

Location: Praza do Obradoiro (next to the cathedral)

The Hostal de los Reyes Católicos was built as a hospice for pilgrims of all categories of wealth and poverty. Its four patios, with cloister-like pillars, fountains, and simple topiary work in box, are as attractive now as when they were first used in the 16th century. If you aren't staying at the Parador, take tea there or have a drink and ask the porter if you may see the patios. It may not always be possible to visit this way; if not, there are tours of the interiors of various buildings arranged by blue-coated guides. Inquire at the tourist office.

Santiago de Compostela: Pazo and Monasterio de San Lorenzo de Trasouto

Location: In the NW of Santiago de Compostela near the university campus on Rúa de San Lorenzo, which as it nears the Rúa do Pombal becomes Rúa da Poza de Bar

open: Mon and Thu, 11am–1pm and 4.30–6.30pm

Further information from:
Hórreo, 19 Bajo, 15702 Santiago de Compostela, La Coruña
Tel: 981 58 39 99
Fax: 981 56 39 24

Nearby sights of interest:
Cathedral; Praza do Obradoiro; Hostal de los Reyes Católicos (see p.36); Praza da Quintana.

There is little information at the tourist office about this gem of a cloister garden. It is an easy walk from the centre of Santiago, or take a taxi. Once you arrive ring the large doorbell long and loud and wait for the gardener who will take you into the monastery, where you can see the church, the sacristy, and the cloisters. The buildings themselves are of great historic interest. The monastery was founded in 1216 and in the 15th century became the property of the Count of Altamira, whose family ceded it to the Franciscans. In the 19th century it came back into the full ownership of the descendants of the Count of Altamira, the Dukes of Soma and of Medina de las Torres. The palace is now used by the family as a private residence and some of the large rooms, the cloisters, and the extensive gardens are used by members of the public for holding banquets, conventions, and other social functions.

The topiary work at the centre of the cloister gardens consists of box, aged 400 years and over 140cm (55in) high. The patterning of the box is said to represent the metal grid on which San Lorenzo

Ancient, closely packed box hedges frame a small grotto and fountain.

(St Lawrence) was burned. Other interpretations suggest it signifies the shell badge worn by pilgrims to Santiago and the cross of St Dominic. So closely has it grown that it is difficult for the gardener to get a ladder and himself in between the rows for the task of cutting it back. Hanging like soft curtains, several ancient wisteria twist along the arches of the cloisters, providing colour, fragrance, and shade in spring and early summer.

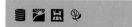

open: By appointment, 1 May to 15 Sep, on first and third Wed of the month; guided tours (with maximum of 25 people in the group)

Further information and to arrange visits:
Jardines Históricos, 39530 Puente San Miguel, Cantabria

Nearby sights of interest:
Town of Santillana del Mar.

26 *La Finca Puente San Miguel*

Location: 3km (2 miles) from Torrelavega, 30km (18½ miles) SW of Santander

There is a fine collection of trees at La Finca Puente San Miguel, many dating from the garden's earliest planting some 250 years ago. Until 1941 the garden boasted the first eucalyptus in northern Spain, but it blew down in that year. Among the stars in this collection are a *Ginkgo biloba*, a dawn redwood, a coastal redwood, one of the largest *Magnolia grandiflora* in Europe, *Cordyline australis*, and a crescent-shaped planting of swamp cypress.

In the 1930s a Sevillian landscape architect was invited to design an area of the garden, and the result is a harmonious fusion of Italianate Renaissance style with an Islamic element centred on water, canals, and fountains. In the mid-1980s Carmen Añon was commissioned to create a futuristic garden near the arboretum and it is this garden, with mirrors and water features, which provides the necessary impetus to carry this 18th-century landscape park into the next century.

Mirror images of the water features are among the modernistic details added in the 20th century.

Parque Natural del Señorío de Bértiz

Location: Near the village of Oieregi on the N121A, which runs between St Jean de Luz and Pamplona; Oieregi is approximately 40km (25 miles) N of Pamplona

A former private estate set in a romantic-style parkland was created during the 1920s by the then owner Pedro Ciga Mayo. The house dates from the 17th century, but the pergolas, chapel, fountains, grottoes, statuary, and viewpoints overlooking the River Bidasoa were the work of Pedro Ciga Mayo.

There are over 126 species of trees and shrubs including many conifers, holm oaks, Spanish chestnuts, and cypresses, and particularly good specimens of swamp cypress, cedar of Lebanon, Himalayan cedars, and *Sequoiadendron giganteum*. The River Bidasoa runs through the property, and there is a gazebo or mirador for enjoying the view across the river. There are two ornamental lakes, adding to the romanticism of the garden. The larger lake, 100m (328ft) long and 15m (49ft) wide at its maximum, has two bridges which lead to a small island. At its widest point this lake is planted with a bamboo thicket and along the shore the flowering shrubs include camellias and azaleas.

open: Daily, April to Sep 10am–2pm and 4–8pm, Oct to Mar 10am–2pm and 4–6pm; no charge for retired people, children under 14, and unemployed

Further information from: Parque Natural del Señorío de Bértiz, 31720 Oieregi, Navarra

Nearby sights of interest: Basque villages; trout streams, the stream-side village of Etxalar, 20km (12½ miles) N of the park.

An intimate small pond with a palm-planted island.

Pazo de Soutomaior

Location: 14km (8¾ miles) S of Pontevedra, off the N550, near the village of Rial

Although known as a *pazo*, Soutomaior is a 15th-century castle. Surrounding it is an expansive estate of some 25ha (62 acres). Much of it is farmed; vines and fruit trees are also grown on the hillsides near the castle. The area close to the granite castle is laid to lawn with large specimen trees, and there is a wooded area a short distance away. Among the trees there are sizeable specimens of sequoia and Lawson's cypresses. There is a box-edged geometric planting near to the castle infilled with bright summer bedding in season. Like many Galician parks it holds a vast collection of camellia species and hybrids. Roses, too, are well represented here, with specimens of climbers such as *Rosa* 'Paul's Scarlet' thriving.

open: Tue to Fri 4–8pm, Sat, Sun, and Public Holidays 11am–1pm and 4–8pm

Further information from: Pontevedra Tourist Office Tel: 986 85 08 14

Nearby sights of interest: Old city, Ourense; Vigo; Misión Botánica de Lourizán (see p.30); Parque Quiñones de León (see p.34).

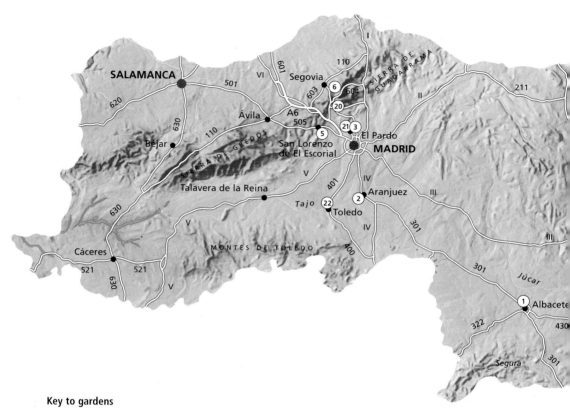

Key to gardens

1 La Rosaleda
2 Jardín de la Isla, Jardín del Parterre, and Jardín del Príncipe
3 La Quinta del Duque de Arco
4 El Huerto del Cura
5 El Escorial
6 Jardines de la Granja de San Ildefonso
7 Invernadero de Arganzuela
8 Estación de Atocha
9 Parque de la Fuente del Berro
10 Parque del Buen Retiro
11 Casa de Campo

12 Parque Juan Carlos I
13 El Jardín del Palacio de Liria
14 El Campo del Moro
15 Parque del Oeste
16 Parque de la Alameda de Osuna
17 Real Jardín Botánico
18 Jardines de Sabatini

19 Museo de Sorolla
20 La Rosaleda
21 Palacio Real de El Pardo
22 El Cigarral de Menores
23 Jardín Botánico de Valencia
24 El Jardín de Monforte
25 Jardines del Real
26 Jardines del Río Turia

Key

═══ Motorways
─── Principal trunk highways
③ Gardens
⬤ Major towns and cities
• Towns

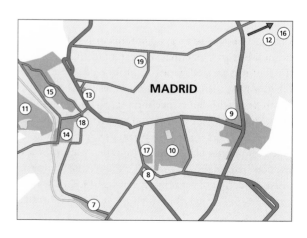

Central Spain

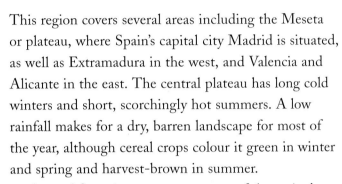

This region covers several areas including the Meseta or plateau, where Spain's capital city Madrid is situated, as well as Extramadura in the west, and Valencia and Alicante in the east. The central plateau has long cold winters and short, scorchingly hot summers. A low rainfall makes for a dry, barren landscape for most of the year, although cereal crops colour it green in winter and spring and harvest-brown in summer.

Around Segovia, en route to some of the region's important garden landscapes of El Escorial (see pp.47–8) and La Granja de San Ildefonso (see pp.48–9), the Guadarrama Mountains support vast beech and oak forests, making glowing autumn displays. In spring, alpines and wildflowers colour the dramatic mountainous landscapes that flank the central plateau.

Madrid, which is in the centre of the country at 787m (2,000ft) above sea level, experiences cold winters, but temperatures never stay below freezing for long. Summers are hot, rising to very hot, with an average temperature of 30–35°C (85–95°F) reaching 48°C (118°F) on occasions. In the city there are numerous public parks and given the high density of

Once a busy terminus, the old Atocha Station is now a plant house.

population, over 3.5 million people, they are welcome outlets for city dwellers to enjoy daily and at weekends. In Parque del Buen Retiro (see p.51), one of the city's oldest parks, known in its early days as a place for courtly and theatrical distractions, entertainment is still the order of the day. Jugglers, clowns, balloon-sellers, and fortune-tellers are there in force at weekends, when occasionally there are even book fairs.

Fountains in all the main public squares, linear parks, and flower-sellers at the centre of major city thorough-fares, such as the Avenida de la Ilustración, add to the floral attractions of Madrid. For centuries the gardens at the Palacio Real in Aranjuez (see pp.44–5) have been a magnet for citizens of Madrid as a green, cool place offering fresh countryside air.

Across the central region at the coast near Valencia and Alicante are gardens with totally different characters. The climate in the Levante, as the region which includes the provinces of Valencia and Alicante is known, is Mediterranean (like that of its northern neighbour, Cataluña). Rainfall is low except for the autumn when there are likely to be floods. Olives, vines, and almonds are among the crops that grow well here naturally. In winter, during January and February, almond blossoms turn the landscape into a sea of pink and white and in spring, during March and April, the cherry trees in the higher valley areas bloom. Irrigation has led to the introduction of other crops including vast expanses of citrus orchards.

Vine-growing or market gardening on *huertas* (irrigated areas) are the occupation of the majority of farmers, and gardening as such is not a high priority. However, there are number of important gardens including El Huerto del Cura at Elche (see p.47).

Jardines del Real in Valencia evolved from a Royal Park into a public park and municipal nursery.

Part of this vast plantation of 300,000 palm trees, said to have been planted by the Phoenicians around 300BC, has been enclosed and is open to the public.

In Valencia there are two old gardens, El Jardín de Monforte (see p.64) and the Jardín Botánico (see p.63), worth visiting for their past, as well as the future restorations planned for them. One of Spain's most forward-thinking 20th-century landscape architects, Ricardo Bofill, and his associates of the Taller de Arquitectura, designed and constructed the neoclassical Jardines del Río Turia (see p.65). The gardens fill a section of the dry river bed of the now diverted River Turia.

The warmth of the Costa Blanca, the Costa del Azahar, and the Costa Cálida has encouraged a vast tourist industry and the growth of a more or less permanent expatriate community made up of sun-loving Europeans from northern temperate zones. They are keen gardeners and meet regularly, visiting members' private gardens and others open to the public. They also hold lectures and would welcome visits from garden tourists to the area (contact the local tourist office for details).

The stone wall cascade at the Parque de la Fuente del Berro is a dramatic, naturalistic feature.

From the garden of the Casita del Principe there are glimpses of the roofscape of the Escorial monastery.

Albacete: La Rosaleda

Location: W of the city centre in Jardines de la Fiesta del Árbol

open: All year, daily, dawn to dusk

Further information from:
Departamento de Parques y Jardines, Ayuntamiento, Albacete

Nearby sights of interest:
Surrounding countryside.

Set within the larger public park of Jardines de la Fiesta del Arbol is a recently created formal rose garden, La Rosaleda. Arranged to a circular plan with rows of roses, rippling out from a central plaza, it features hundreds of modern and old roses. A double pergola on the outer rims of the rose garden holds climbing and rambling roses.

Aranjuez: Jardín de la Isla, Jardín del Parterre, and Jardín del Príncipe

Location: Jardín de la Isla and Jardín del Parterre are close to the Palacio Real; Jardín del Príncipe is about 2km (1¼ miles) away from the palace, on the Calle de la Reina; an old steam train runs between Madrid and Aranjuez

open: All year, daily, 10am to dusk
open: As above; admission charge

Further information from:
Aranjuez Tourist Office, Plaza de San Antonio, 9, Aranjuez
Tel: 91 891 04 27

Nearby sights of interest:
Palacio Real (closes Mon); Iglesia de San Antonio; Iglesia de Alpajés (oldest church in Aranjuez); Casa de Oficios y Caballeros, and Casa de Infantes (lodgings of servants and visitors to the Court); Casa del Labrador (Labourer's House, closes Mon); Casa de Marinos (Mariners' House, closes Mon) in the grounds of the Jardín del Príncipe.

Grass and bright bedding plants line the Parterre Garden.

Recreation has always been part of Aranjuez's attraction. Felipe II (1556–98) established a palace and gardens on the site around a medieval hunting ground. In the 18th century Felipe V (1700–46), together with his French gardeners, headed by successive generations of the Boutelou family, created veritable pleasure grounds in the Jardín de la Isla and the Jardín del Parterre, while Carlos IV (1788–1808) was responsible for the Jardín del Príncipe.

Although hunting is no longer the recreation on offer at Aranjuez, the gardens, with their mature trees and shady walks along the banks of the River Tajo (Tagus), offer a welcome respite from soaring summer temperatures to *Madrileños*, tourists, and citizens of Aranjuez alike. It is a popular place and it may be better to visit on a weekday rather than a weekend. In addition to its romantic gardens, there are many important monuments to see.

The gardens here have been the inspiration for many of Spain's artists. A walk in these gardens in the cool of a summer's evening is said to be the well-spring for Joaquín Rodrigo's *Concierto de Aranjuez*.

The trio of gardens at Aranjuez are spread over a large area, around 300ha (741 acres), and would take days to explore fully. But in a day it is possible to take in the Jardín del Parterre and some areas of the Jardín de la Isla before or after a tour of the palace. Then take the *chiquitren* (a bone-shaking experience over the cobbled streets, disconcertingly accompanied by a recording of the *Concierto de Aranjuez*) on a round trip, on which there are selected stops where you can embark or disembark. Closest to the Palacio Real in the Jardín del Parterre is a small parterre dating from the reign of Felipe II (1556–98). This was recently excavated and restored and its several geometric beds hold linear and curved plantings of box, each with a fruit tree at the centre. The main French-style parterre garden dating from the 18th century has the River Tagus on its northern side. It was the work of Don Esteban Boutelou the Elder, one of a number of French gardeners employed by the Bourbon king Felipe V. It is a pleasant garden to walk through with well-kept lawns, colourful summer bedding, and avenues of mature *Magnolia grandiflora*. There are two pools with white marble statuary and fountains representing Hercules and Ceres, respectively, in the parterre. Classical-style urns on stone balustrades around the garden, or on plinths, hold brightly coloured plants. They have replaced the original stylish and colourful ceramic pots made at the Alcora potteries in Valencia.

From the parterre you cross a canal that takes water from the river alongside the palace and enter the Jardín de la Isla. These gardens, dating from the 16th century, are on a man-made island. Here there are many interlinked areas or courts, hedged with box or hornbeam, dating from the 18th century. Avenues lead into courtyards or tree-shaded seating areas, with statuary and fountains representing mythological figures. The biggest and most dramatic of these is the Fountain of Hercules. The largest court area is set around a statue of a boy taking a thorn out of his foot, known as the Harpies Fountain. The trees, including horse chestnuts, limes, and planes, are of great size and age.

The Jardín del Príncipe (a ten-minute walk from the palace) is a wooded parkland of 150ha (371 acres). Work began on it between 1746 and 1759 but it was under Carlos IV and his architect Juan de Villanueva that much of the building work and structure of the garden was put into place, and it was named in his honour. Work finished on the garden in 1804. The influence of the English landscape movement of the 18th century was paramount, with romantic and rustic houses, pavilions, and grottoes being added to the garden. Still remaining are a group of pavilions in the Jardín de los Pabellones (Garden of the Summer Houses) near the river side; Casa de Marinos (Mariners' House), now a museum housing sumptuously decorated river boats that were once used by the royal family, and the Casa del Labrador (Labourer's House), which is sometimes used by the royal family today.

The route to the Mariners' House follows the river, offering glimpses of the buildings on the far bank. Pomegranates grow against the walls of several pavilions.

open: All year, Mon to Sat
10.30am–6pm, Sun and Public
Holidays 10am–2pm

Further information from:
Patrimonio Nacional
Tel: 91 376 03 29

Nearby sights of interest:
Palacio Real de El Pardo
(see p.62).

Pencil-thin Italian cypresses look
like architectural features against
the yellow-ochre walls of the
upper terraces.

La Quinta del Duque de Arco

Location: About 11km (7 miles) N of Madrid, 3km (2 miles) from the Carretera de El Pardo on the C605

A few kilometres from the Palacio Real de El Pardo (see p.62), La Quinta del Duque de Arco is a small hunting lodge which is undergoing restoration. The building and gardens became royal property in 1745 when they were given to Felipe V (1700–46). The garden has been restored in recent times to its former neoclassical origins. Even so, some paintwork is peeling from the walls and some of the statuary is a little fragile-looking.

The garden is on two levels, each with a central pool and fountain. The upper pool is backed by a wall with statuary, urns, and shaped junipers, which make eerie reflections in the pool. Huge specimens of Wellingtonia (*Sequoiadendron giganteum*) grow at the centre of the low-growing box-edged parterres of the upper level. A cascade is the main feature of the pool on the lower terrace. The informal, grotto-like stonework on this level contrasts with the neoclassical style of the upper terrace. The views around the garden are of the open country, which has been a royal hunting ground for centuries.

Elche: El Huerto del Cura

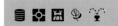

Location: On the eastern side of the city centre

At Elche, El Palmeral, the grove of ancient *Phoenix dactylifera* palms, numbering between 300,000 and 400,000, is a magnificent sight. The Phoenicians are said to be responsible for planting them in 300BC. Part of the plantation, which surrounds Elche on three sides, has been enclosed and is known as El Huerto del Cura (the Curate's Orchard). The curate referred to is José Mariá Castaño, a priest from Elche, who probably used it as a date orchard. Now it supports many of the typical Mediterranean orchard crops such as carob, jujube, lemon, pomegranate, and orange. The orchards and the palm plantation within El Huerto were restored in the 1940s and again recently.

Many attractive flowering plants including strelitzia and arum lilies grow in various beds, while the cheese plant, *Monstera deliciosa*, grows either as ground cover or up tree trunks. The most exotic specimen is the Imperial palm tree, named as such by Castaño in honour of the visit of the Empress Elizabeth of Austria in 1894. It has eight trunks and is often described as a huge candelabra. All over the orchard are trees with inscriptions dedicated to famous people who have visited the garden, including the present King and Queen of Spain and the pianist Artur Rubinstein. There are also two water features, a large natural pond and a small formal pool.

open: Daily, summer 9am–8.30pm and winter 9am–6pm

Further information from:
Heurto del Cura, Porta de la Morera 49, 03203 Elche, Alicante
Tel: 967 45 19 36

Nearby sights of interest:
Basílica de Santa María;
Museo Arquelógico.

The Imperial palm has eight trunks.

 # El Escorial

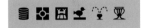

Location: 50km (31 miles) NW of Madrid

There are many compelling reasons for visiting El Escorial, which was planned by Felipe II as a monastery and tomb and completed in 1584. El Escorial, on the foothills of the Sierra de Guadarrama, was the largest Spanish building of the Renaissance period and today it still dominates the landscape, with its spare style and glimmering slate roof. You can tour the monastery at your own pace, but if gardens are part of the reason for visiting there are several within the monastery itself and two attached to the small 18th-century palaces or *casitas*.

The main cloister, Patio de los Evangelistas, is an example of a very pure and geometric style with square parterres hedged in box and four pools at its centre. The meeting of the pathways within the patio is marked by an octagonal, domed building housing sculptures of the Evangelists. It can only be visited with special permission obtained in advance by letter.

open: 15 Apr to 15 Oct, Tue to Sun, 10am–1.30pm and 3.30–6.30pm; 16 Oct to 14 Apr, Tue to Sun, 10am–1.30pm and 3–6pm; closes Public Holidays; Jardín de los Frailes: Apr to Sep 10am–7pm, Oct to Mar 10am–6pm
open: As above but in winter 10am–1.30pm and 4–6pm; admission charge but free entry Wed to EC citizens

Further information from:
Tourist Office, c/Floridablanca, 10, San Lorenzo de El Escorial
Tel: 91 890 15 54

Nearby sights of interest:
Segovia (aqueduct, castle).

On the southern side of the monastery Jardín de los Frailes, a series of geometric parterres with box hedging, stretches along the whole of the southern façade and can be viewed from the Galería de Convalecientes. Below this terrace is a long pool with alcoves holding standard citrus plants. From here the division between built architectural landscape and the rural reality is visible; olive groves with sheep and goats grazing fill the view.

There are two other gardens to visit in the Escorial complex. They are the gardens at the Casita de Arriba (also known as Casita del Infante) and the Casita del Príncipe. The houses are the work of the architect Juan de Villanueva and were built as small recreational palaces for the two eldest sons of Carlos III. The gardens of the Casita del Príncipe are formal and show Villanueva's keen sense of geometric shapes. The box hedges are now shaded by massive Wellingtonias (*Sequoiadendron giganteum*) and other conifers that dominate the gardens at the rear of the lodge. Roses, wisteria, and jasmine climb against walls, while bright pelargoniums fill formal-shaped pottery urns. These geometric hedged gardens at the rear are on two terraces with a sloping walkway up to a lake at the top level. From here the view of the garden, which takes on an embroidered carpet-like dimension, and out across the countryside is dramatic. As you walk through this garden the fragrance of box foliage, citrus flowers, and roses, in season, is as enchanting as the glimpses of the dome of the monastery basilica, which seems to float through the conifer foliage.

Manicured hedges contrast with the towering shapes of mature conifers in Casita del Principe.

open: Tue to Sun, summer 10am–7pm and winter 10am–6.30pm; entry free except when fountains playing

open: Tue to Sun; admission charge; guided tours arranged

Further information from:
Patrimonio Nacional, La Granja de San Ildefonso

Nearby sights of interest:
Palacio Real de la Granja de San Ildefonso; Segovia.

6 *Jardines de la Granja de San Ildefonso*

Location: 11km (7 miles) SE of Segovia on the N601

There are numerous fountains to see and you can wander at will or inspect them like a stamp collector in strict numeric order, following the map available at the entrance. However, opting for this route means you take the long haul up through the woods to the large lake called El Mar (The Sea). It is preferable to progress through the garden in a less ordered way so that you move upwards to the lake, at leisure, and then finally down to the spectacular Fuente de la Fama (the Fountain of Fame), which it is alleged can be seen from Segovia, and Fuente de los Baños de Diana (the Baths of Diana).

Start your visit with the formally bedded-out parterre of closely clipped box hedges and geometric shapes in front of the palace. You can walk under the shade of plane trees to the Fuente de la Selva (Fountain of the Forest) and the ornamental ponds and canals in the lower part of the garden. Then continue along the path to the Anfítrite (Amphitheatre) where the view is dominated by the Cascada Nueva. This fabulous marble staircase of water is as impressive whether viewed from its base or its source. Once you have covered this section, walk up to El Mar and look into its calm waters where the surrounding peaks are mirrored.

Although the design suggests formality it becomes clear when walking through the garden that La Granja has a more relaxed feel. Even if fountains are not playing, their statuary and artistry are consummate: many are cast in bronze, while others are carved in marble. Felipe V commissioned great sculptors of the day, mostly from France, including René Frémin and Jean Thierry, to make this water extravaganza. Once you are out of the neatness of the setpiece parterres a beguiling network of paths, geometric and axial on the plan, shaded and softened by large-scale plantings of Scots pines (*Pinus sylvestris*), Pyrenean oak (*Quercus pyrenaica*), linden, chestnut, and hedges of beech and hornbeam, tempt you into further excursions.

The dramatic Cascada Nueva descends to a pool just above Fuente de la Anfítrite.

The fountains play from the end of March (or from Easter, if it is earlier) until August and on Saturdays, Sundays, and Public Holidays in September depending on the water supply. It is only on a few days in summer that all major fountains explode with their liquid firework display. Apart from the excitement of the water spectacular, the crowd's reaction is fun to watch in itself. Spectators position them-selves at the starting fountain and rush from it to the next and the next, to see the water whoosh out of the pipes.

 # *Madrid: Invernadero de Arganzuela*

Location: In the Arganzuela park in the SW of the city; nearest underground station Pirámides

open: Tue to Fri, summer 11am–2pm and 5–8.30pm, winter 10am–2pm and 5–7.30pm; arrive 30 minutes before closing time or you will not be admitted

A bit off the beaten track, this recently renovated former industrial building stands on land belonging to the old El Matadero slaughter house. It is interesting for its glass and iron structure, as well as for the collection of plants it holds. Thousands of plants from many continents are well established in several areas, which each provides a different microclimate. It is also known by locals as Palacio de Cristal (Crystal Palace).

Further information from:
Departamento de Parques y Jardines, Ayuntamiento de Madrid, Calle Mayor 69, 28013 Madrid
Tel: 91 588 29 00

Nearby sights of interest:
Parque Tierno Galván.

open: All year, daily,
7am–11.30pm

Further information from:
Departamento de Parques y
Jardines, Ayuntamiento de Madrid,
Calle Mayor 69, 28013 Madrid
Tel: 91 588 29 00

Nearby sights of interest:
Museo del Prado; Parque del Buen
Retiro (see opposite); Centro de
Arte Reina Sofía.

Madrid: Estación de Atocha

Location: Plaza del Emperador Carlos V; nearest underground Atocha

Built of wrought iron and glass the old Atocha Station, housing Madrid's first train service to Aranjuez (1851), now replaced by a modern terminus, is the ideal setting for an imaginative indoor tropical garden. Several raised beds are the habitats for a wide range of plants that enjoy humid glasshouse conditions.

Flowering plants, including agapanthus, species begonia, and clivia, brighten the beds in season. In the main the beds contain evergreens such as bamboo, shefflera, and ground-covering plants including pilea and creeping fig (*Ficus pumila*), which also swarms up the many palm trunks. Palms, such as coconut and phoenix, provide a change of height. All these plants offer tranquil and pleasant surroundings to travellers en route to the new station, as well as to visitors simply enjoying a drink and snack at the restaurants and bars that have taken over the former station.

---

open: At all times

Further information from:
Departamento de Parques
y Jardines, Ayuntamiento de
Madrid, Calle Mayor 69,
28013 Madrid
Tel: 91 588 29 00

Nearby sights of interest:
Museo Arqueológico Nacional;
Parque del Buen Retiro (see
opposite); Museo de la Moneda.

**Brightly coloured summer bedding
at the park's entrance.**

Madrid: Parque de la Fuente del Berro

Location: E of the city centre, two entrances, Calle Enrique D'Almonte and Calle de los Peñascales; nearest underground O'Donnell

The park takes its name from the springs and fountains which led to it becoming a royal property in the 17th century, when Felipe IV bought it from Benedictine monks. Through his purchase Felipe reserved the rights over the water for the royal household. Fuente del Rey, the fountain with sparkling drinking water which was so celebrated, is just outside the existing park at the Calle de los Peñascales entrance. Although evocative it is often unkempt and rubbish-strewn.

In the 18th century the park and its waters passed out of royal ownership and eventually, in 1948, it was bought by the City of Madrid. Described as "in the romantic style" it is a little known park, slightly off the beaten track, but worth visiting for its good collection of trees, winding intimate paths, and its dramatic cobble-wall cascade. At the entrance peacocks strut around a circular pool with classical urns and bright summer bedding. Among the interesting pieces of statuary are those in homage to Pushkin, the poet Bécquer, and the musician Iniesta. Wellingtonias (*Sequoiadendron giganteum*), crape myrtle (*Lagerstroemia indica*), strawberry tree (*Arbutus unedo*), and cork oak (*Quercus suber*) are among the specimens growing in the park.

10 *Madrid: Parque del Buen Retiro*

Location: In central Madrid, with several entrances on Avenida de Menéndez Pelayao, Calle de O'Donnell, Calle de Alcalá, Calle de Alfonso XII, and Calle del Poeta Esteban de Villegas

In a crowded city like Madrid the Parque del Buen Retiro or del Retiro offers air, light, and, because of its size – 120ha (296 acres) – a sense of space and the possibility of total relaxation.

Buen Retiro is like a day book that can be dipped into from time to time, and will always offer entertainment. For a roughly round trip enter at the Puerta de la América Española and walk past the artificial Colina de los Gatos (Mountain of the Cats). Turn right at Paseo del Salvador and then left at Paseo Duque Fernán Núñez. All the while you will be walking through densely planted, wood-like areas. Eventually you will come to Jardines de Cecilio Rodríguez and if you turn left along the Paseo de Uruguay you will find a rose garden modelled on La Bagatelle in Paris. Before turning right up the Avenida de Cuba, look for the only public statue in the world to the devil in the Plaza del Angel Caído (Fallen Angel). If you wander to the right, off the Avenida de Cuba, you will find the 19th-century Palacio de Cristal (Crystal Palace), a confection in iron and glass. In front of it is a lake, with a fountain and a damp grotto tunnel. Swamp cypresses thrive in the water and make a beautiful display in autumn.

To enjoy the sight of El Estanque, walk along Salón del Estanque. Boats can be hired and along this route in the park anything can happen. There are all sorts of sideshows including fortune-tellers, jugglers, stilt-walkers, balloon-sellers, and, of course, promenading *Madrileños*, enjoying their park.

Filmshows, concerts, and fairs fill the park with life on summer evenings. All this and plants too. As you stroll in search of the focal points, the plants become a subtle background. Wellingtonias, yews, avenues of planes, elms, horse chestnuts, poplars, and pines are dominant. If you leave by the entrance near Puerta de Alcalá, enjoy the Fuente de los Galápagos (Fountain of the Turtles). Within the park itself there are many fountains.

open: At all times

open: Travelling art exhibitions in Palacio de Velázquez, Palacio de Cristal, and Casa de Vacas: all year, Tue to Sat 10am–2pm and 5–7pm, Sun 10am–2pm

Further information from:
Departamento de Parques y Jardines, Ayuntamiento de Madrid, Calle Mayor 69, 28013 Madrid
Tel: 91 588 29 00

Nearby sights of interest:
Real Jardín Botánico (see pp.56–9); Parque de la Fuente del Berro (see opposite); Museo del Prado; District of Salamanca; Museo Arqueológico Nacional; Museo Thyssen-Bornemisza; Museo del Ejército.

A fountain and pool in the rose garden, which is modelled on La Bagatelle in Paris.

11

Madrid: Casa de Campo

Location: Avenida de Portugal, to the W of Madrid; nearest undergrounds Batán, Lago, Norte

open: All year, daily, various attractions have fixed hours; free entry to parkland, but admission charges for various attractions

Further information from:
Departamento de Parques y Jardines, Ayuntamiento de Madrid, Calle Mayor 69, 28013 Madrid
Tel: 91 588 29 00

Nearby sights of interest:
Parque de Atracciones; Zoo.

Created and used as a royal hunting park by Felipe II in 1560, today the Casa de Campo forms a green lung between the city and the northern suburbs. It covers 1,740ha (4,300 acres) and has a main road running through it. The roadside area is somewhat disconcerting, as soliciting is carried out here. However, the park is large enough for every call that is made on it, and its pine-covered, scrubby landscape offers interest in every season.

There is a huge boating lake with a constantly playing geyser-like fountain and from here there are clear views of the Madrid skyline. Specimens of cedar, elm, holly, horse chestnut, oak, pine, black poplar, and yew are among the notable trees. The locust tree, *Gleditsia japonica*, and plane trees offer shade in summer and attractive leaf colour in autumn.

12

Madrid: Parque Juan Carlos I

Location: Near Madrid's permanent Trade Fair Centre on the eastern rim of the outer city, near the airport; take bus 122 from Arturo Soria underground

open: All year, daily, dawn to dusk

Further information from:
Departamento de Parques y Jardines, Ayuntamiento de Madrid, Calle Mayor 69, 28013 Madrid
Tel: 91 588 29 00

Nearby sights of interest:
Parque de la Alameda de Osuna (see p.55).

One of the many modern sculptures in this exciting park.

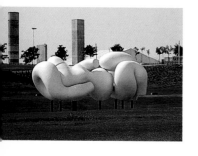

Parque Juan Carlos I is one of Madrid's most modern and exciting outdoor spaces. It is not on the regular tourist route as it is out of the city between the airport and centre and, therefore, omitted. It is a dramatic contrast to the 18th-century romanticism of the Parque de la Alameda de Osuna (see p.55). The Parque Juan Carlos I was opened in May 1992 and although the vegetation has yet to mature, the excitement of large expanses of water in the form of lakes, canals, and rivers, modern sculpture, grass pyramids, and sweeping lawns, as well as sports facilities, is enough to attract hordes of *Madrileños* to the park.

It is large enough, at 220ha (544 acres), for everyone to have fun and not feel overcrowded. The park is surrounded by a ring of olive trees, making a circle 1km (¾ mile) in diameter. At the centre of the park is the Jardín de las Tres Culturas, so-called because it celebrates the three traditions – Judaism, Christianity, and Islam – which together constitute so much of Spain's cultural heritage. *Son et lumière* spectacles are offered and there is a way-marked route across and around the water features. The Parque Juan Carlos I is a place to explore, to picnic in, and to spend time understanding its modern design and attributes.

13 *Madrid: El Jardín del Palacio de Liria*

Location: In the NW of the old town, Calle Princesa 20

open: By appointment in advance

Further information from:
Fundación Casa de Alba, Calle Princesa 20, 28008 Madrid
Tel: 91 247 53 02

Completed by Ventura Rodríguez, one of the notable architects of the late 18th century, Palacio de Liria has been the residence of successive generations of the influential and wealthy Dukes of Alba since it was built. In front of the palace specimen trees, such as box, holly, cedar, and magnolias, offer an informal wooded feeling to the sweeping driveway.

The way to the more formal gardens on the northern side of the palace takes you past an ornate fountain alcove and up a flight of stairs. From here you can view the *parterre de broderie* of closely clipped box hedging and large sentinel yews, pruned into geometric shapes, the early 20th-century work of J C N Forestier. A central pool with classical statuary and a fountain in white marble is part of his design. Formal stairways with sphinx-like statuary lead to a terrace lined by a long iron pergola, covered by ancient, twining stems of wisteria. From the pergola terrace you can see the formal garden, as well as catch glimpses of the flower-filled borders above the terrace.

On a walkway to the west of the terrace is a line of dog graves, some of them dating back centuries, which are a poignant memorial to the domestic pets of the Alba family.

Nearby sights of interest:
Collection of art, including tapestry belonging to the Alba family (open Sat but only by appointment; apply for permission to visit in advance); Museo Cerralbo; Malasaña quarter with old houses; Templo de Debod (see p.54).

The formally clipped parterre punctuated by shaped yews behind the palace. A fountain and pool add to the garden's intimacy.

open: All year, daily, 10am–8pm; closes 6pm winter; gardens closed when official receptions held at palace

Further information from:
Patrimonio Nacional
Tel: 91 542 00 59

Nearby sights of interest:
Jardines de Sabatini (see p.60).

14 Madrid: El Campo del Moro

Location: Entrance on Paseo Virgen del Puerto to the W of the old town

El Campo del Moro (Field of the Moor) is a 20ha (49acre) park to the west of the old quarter of Madrid. It takes its name from the Moorish army of Ali Ben Yusuf which camped here in 1109. In the 17th century, under Felipe IV, the gardens were used for hunting. Isabel II, in the early part of the 19th century, transformed the hilly ground into a garden and park, introducing formal flowerbeds and the two main promenades. She also arranged for the construction of a camellia house and ordered the installation of the two major fountains in the gardens, the Fountain of the Tritons and the Fountain of the Shells.

In the late 19th century, Queen María Cristina made further improvements and the park and gardens were landscaped in what the Spanish describe as "the English style", characterized by winding paths, sweeping lawns, woodland, statuary, and fountains.

The most dramatic view of the garden is from the Paseo Virgen del Puerto entrance, where your eye moves up a massive sweep of lawn to the façade of the Palacio Real. To the right and left of this expanse there are walks along paths overhung by avenues of planes and horse chestnuts. At the end of one of the main axial paths is an arcade of juniper clipped into arches and hedges.

---

open: All year, daily, dawn to dusk

Further information from:
Departamento de Parques y Jardines, Ayuntamiento de Madrid, Calle Mayor 69, 28013 Madrid
Tel: 91 588 29 00

Nearby sights of interest:
Templo de Debod (see right); Palacio Real; Jardines de Sabatini (see p.60); El Campo del Moro (see above); El Jardín del Palacio de Liria (see p.53); Ermita de San Antonio de la Florida (Goya's frescos).

15 Madrid: Parque del Oeste

Location: To the W of the city centre with several entrances

Parque del Oeste covers about 98ha (242 acres) of land on a sloping site above the River Manzanares. Many features of the 17th and 18th century were destroyed during the Civil War when the park was stormed by the citizens. It was restored and new components added in the mid-20th century. The rose garden is of particular interest. It is a wonderful sight in early summer when the hundreds of modern roses, in their serried ranks, bloom.

Some parts of the park are densely covered with elm and horse chestnuts, others are more open, but from most parts of it there are good views over Madrid and towards the Casa de Campo (see p.52), just across the river. The 4th-century BC Egyptian temple, the Templo de Debod, that was given to Spain as thanks to the Spanish engineers involved in the Aswan Dam project, lies here and, although it looks incongruous at first, it makes its own dramatic impact on the park's landscape.

16 *Madrid: Parque de la Alameda de Osuna*

Location: E of Madrid off the N11 motorway; entrance off Avenida de America on the Paseo de la Alameda, in Barajas district; nearest underground Canillejas

open: Sat, Sun, and Public Holidays, 1 Apr to 30 Sep 9am–9pm and 1 Oct to 30 Mar 9am–6.30pm

Further information from:
Departamento de Parques y Jardines, Ayuntamiento de Madrid, Calle Mayor 69, 28013 Madrid
Tel: 91 588 29 00

Nearby sights of interest:
Parque Juan Carlos I (see p.52).

Once in a more rural setting, this delightful late 18th-century garden is also known as El Capricho (The Whim or Caprice) de la Alameda de Osuna. Today with local sports fields butting right up to it and a motorway barely a kilometre away, it is less easy to appreciate the romantic and intellectual elements that remain of this fragile landscape. That apart it is a garden worth the search because of its intrinsic qualities and historic value. For its creator, the Duchess of Osuna, it represented her liberal and reforming views and ideas, and was the seat of her salon. The garden had more than ornament as its aim; its objective was to be a place for instruction and one of the most important features was the classical-style building that housed the apiary. Here the duchess' visitors could watch the bees at their work through a glass viewing panel, and take lessons from nature.

There is a formal garden with a parterre in front of the neoclassical palace. One of the restored features is a classical exedra which once held a bronze statue of the Duchess of Osuna, surrounded by sphinxes. Avenues of mature horse chestnuts, elm, pines, and oak give a woodland look to the informal, winding paths. There is a Temple of Bacchus, a hermitage, a boat house, a lake with an artificial island, and a rustic house, Casa de la Vieja.

The restored exedra lacks much of the original statuary.

17 *Madrid: Real Jardín Botánico*

open: All year, daily, 10am; closes 9pm summer and 6pm winter; closes 25 Dec and 1 Jan

Further information from:
Real Jardín Botánico, Plaza de Murillo 2, 281014 Madrid
Tel: 91 420 30 17

Nearby sights of interest:
Museo del Prado; Museo de Artes Decorativas; Museo Nacional de Etnología; Parque del Buen Retiro (see p.51).

Location: Plaza de Murillo 2, S of the Museo del Prado; nearest underground Atocha

Madrid's first royal botanic garden was created at the instigation of Fernando VI in the mid-18th century and was sited on the banks of the River Manzanares. It held a collection of over 2,000 plants obtained by the botanist-surgeon José Quer during his travels, or in exchange with other European botanists.

In 1774 Carlos III moved the Jardín Botánico to its present location and it was opened in 1781. Its building was under the direction of Sabatini, the king's architect, and Juan de Villanueva, the architect responsible for the Museo del Prado and many other of Madrid's museums and historic buildings.

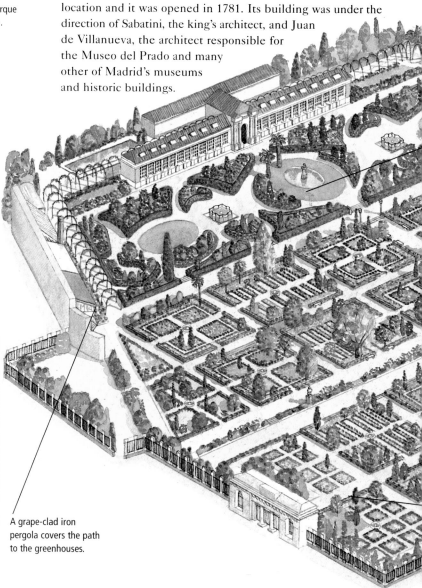

A grape-clad iron pergola covers the path to the greenhouses.

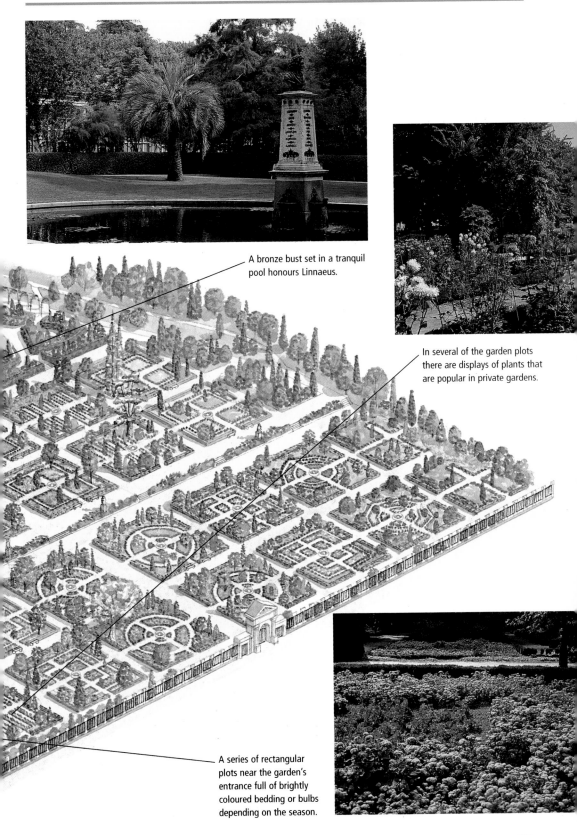

A bronze bust set in a tranquil pool honours Linnaeus.

In several of the garden plots there are displays of plants that are popular in private gardens.

A series of rectangular plots near the garden's entrance full of brightly coloured bedding or bulbs depending on the season.

57

The Real Jardín Botánico underwent periods of great activity when large collections of seeds and plants were introduced, especially those sent from the Spanish colonies in the Americas and the Philippines. The King himself financed plant-collecting expeditions to Peru, Chile, Columbia, and Mexico, and herbaria were compiled. In the late 19th and early 20th centuries, however, the garden was neglected.

Its scientific integrity was maintained by successive directors, but they could not withstand loss of land (1882), for the construction of the building which now houses the Ministry of Agriculture, and the ravages of nature in the shape of a cyclone in 1886, which destroyed over 500 of the garden's most important trees. In 1932 the garden was declared an "Artistic Garden", and in 1974 it was closed to the public and a major restoration was carried out by Leandro Silva Delgado among others. The garden was reopened in 1981 coinciding with its bicentenary.

Much of the original layout was retained and many of the important surviving plants remain. The garden is divided into several distinct areas or terraces. Although the character of each terrace is different, there is a unity provided by the wide paths, the well-proportioned staircases, and the bowl-like granite pools with fountains, placed at regular intervals along the paths. Cool stone benches also set along the paths are particularly welcome on a hot summer's day.

The collection of old roses is held in a quartet of gardens, divided into smaller segments.

The whole garden is very sheltered, ringed by wrought-iron fencing, and heavily planted with evergreen hedging. This rim of shelter makes for a still atmosphere within the garden, which

traps and holds the perfume of roses, aromatic plants, and flowering shrubs such as Japanese mock orange (*Pittosporum tobira*), which quite overpowers the visitor.

Shade throughout comes from a collection of mature and important trees such as tree of heaven (*Ailanthus altissima*), cork oaks, camphor trees, eucalyptus, mulberry, olives, European field elm (*Ulmus minor*), and walnut. Judas trees, pomegranates and the nettle tree, in several species, are well represented. The crape myrtle, *Lagerstroemia indica*, and another member of the myrtle family, *Metrosideros excelsa*, are among species from China.

The first or lower terrace, called The Terrace of Plots, consists of uniformly-shaped beds or plots holding garden, medicinal, aromatic, and culinary plants. An old rose collection, plants endemic to Spain and Portugal, and edible and economically useful plants complete this section. In the next, The Terrace of the Botanical Schools, plants are arranged in their families and one can walk from areas holding the most primitive plant forms to those with the more highly evolved plant groups. The Terrace of "Plano de la Flor" is the oldest part of the garden and was remodelled in the 19th century by the then Director, Mariano de la Paz Graells. At the back of the garden the Villanueva Pavilion is used for charity functions and fund-raising events.

Whether you visit all the areas with a scientific purpose or simply wander through the garden, enjoying its fragrance and beauty, there is a sense of calm and timelessness in this oasis in the midst of a busy part of Madrid.

Grasses offer their ornamental beauty in the Terrace of the Botanical Schools, where plants are arranged in botanical orders.

Tranquillity and symmetry are on offer from the steady progression of pools along box-edged paths.

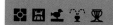

open: At all times

Further information from:
Departamento de Parques y
Jardines, Ayuntamiento de Madrid,
Calle Mayor 69, 28013 Madrid
Tel: 91 588 29 00

Nearby sights of interest:
Plaza de Oriente; Palacio Real;
Nuestra Señora de la Almudena;
El Campo del Moro (see p.54).

Neatly clipped box, sentinel
cypresses, and water features are
the most important elements here.

18 *Madrid: Jardines de Sabatini*

Location: Near Palacio Real, on Cuesta de San Vicente and Plaza de Oriente in NW of old town

Jardines de Sabatini are formal gardens created in the 1930s and named in honour of the 18th-century Italian architect, Francesco Sabatini, responsible for many of Madrid's most impressive buildings and monuments, including the Puerta de Alcalá and the 18th-century extension to Palacio de El Pardo. Built on the site of the old palace stables, they command a good view over Madrid and, in particular, El Campo del Moro (see p.54).

Arranged on a terrace the gardens blend the geometric shapes of closely clipped box hedges with a square pool and fountain. Statuary is accentuated by the statuesque, architectural forms of clipped cypresses. Near the pool the angularity is broken by the irregular shapes of four Spanish firs, *Abies pinsapo*. There are several other pools and fittingly there is an equestrian statue of Carlos III, the monarch who used Sabatini's skills so well in Madrid during the 18th century.

The gardens are near enough to the site of the Plaza de Oriente to be virtually linked. The Plaza de Oriente, the impressive square situated in front of the Palacio Real, is part of a major underground development, so has lost its plants for the present. When it is restored the two gardens will once again soften the façades and plazas around the palace.

---

open: All year, Tue to Sat
10am–3pm and Sun 10am–2pm
open: As above; admission
charge

Further information from:
Museo de Sorolla, Paseo
del General Martínez
Campos 37, Madrid
Tel: 91 310 15 84

Nearby sights of interest:
Paseo de la Castellana; Museo
Lázaro Galdiano.

19 *Madrid: Museo de Sorolla*

Location: Paseo del General Martínez Campos 37

The Museo de Sorolla was the home and studio of the Valencian post-impressionist painter Joaquín Sorolla Bastida (1863–1923), known for his portrait paintings of Spanish people and for his limpid beach scenes. Sorolla employed the Spanish architect E N Repulles to design the house, which was built in 1920, and he designed and built the garden, a cool and shady haven, to house his collection of fountains and fonts. He incorporated coloured ceramic tiles, terracotta, and marble to create a southern Andalusian garden, influenced greatly by his enjoyment of the Alhambra and Generalife (see pp.74–7). The garden is not large but there is a sense of space and distance. Wherever possible he used tiles for decoration – on doors, seats, the rims of pools, and in the paths and patios.

The first garden you enter once through the street gate is influenced by Jardines de los Reales Alcázares in Seville (see p.83). Enclosed by high walls, with statuary and a marble font playing gently, it offers a welcome respite from the busy road outside. Aspidistras in pots, roses, myrtle, and box are the main plants in this part of the garden. The house is covered in places with climbing roses and an old wisteria.

In the second garden the mood changes to the Moorish Spain of Granada. The main feature is a channel of water, lined with terracotta pots of bright geraniums, with jets of water hopping across it. Further into the garden there is a tranquil pool at ground level, which almost invites the weary visitor to cool off beside it. All through the garden are the delightful tilework benches that once graced many Spanish gardens.

The famous water fountain at the Generalife in Granada was the inspiration for Sorolla's Moorish-style garden.

20 *Manzanares el Real: La Rosaleda*

Location: In the Urbanización Peña el Gato, Manzanares el Real, 40km (25 miles) from Madrid on the road to Colmenar Viejo and Miraflores

Rose enthusiast and international judge Señor Angel Esteban González has put together a collection of 700 different roses. Arches support rambling roses and the site itself, high in the Sierra de Guadarrama, offers extraordinary views.

The best time for visiting, of course, is in May when the roses are at their peak, though later in the summer the repeat-flowering and late-flowering varieties are also exceptional.

Señor Esteban has laid the rose garden out to take advantage of the site's natural beauty, and he has planned the walks through it so that the visitor enjoys the roses at their peak.

open: By appointment, contact owner at least two days in advance; rose season mid-Apr to end Sep, depending on weather

Further information from:
Señor Angel Esteban González, c/Pamplona 21, Madrid 28039
Tel: 91 853 03 45 (Manzanares el Real) or 91 459 52 33 (Madrid)

Nearby sights of interest:
Palacio Real de El Pardo; Sierra Centro de Guadarrama; Manzanares el Real; La Pedriza; Colmenar Viejo.

Palacio Real de El Pardo

Location: 11km (7 miles) N of Madrid, close to the main square in El Pardo

open: All year, Mon to Sat
10.30am–6pm and Sun and
Public Holidays 10am–2pm
open: All year, Wed to Mon
10am–12.30pm and 3–5.30pm,
Sun 10am–1pm

Further information from:
Patrimonio Nacional
Tel: 91 376 03 29

Nearby sights of interest:
La Quinta del Duque de Arco
(see p.46); Palacio Real de El
Pardo (combined ticket for
Casita del Príncipe).

The town owes its existence to the successive Royal palaces
built here by Felipe II and Felipe III. There are vast tracts of
holm oak forest around the palace and it is as a base for hunting
that it had its origins. The first of many successive palaces was
built here in the reign of Enrique II (1369–79). During the 20th
century General Franco made it his official residence. Latterly
it has been used by foreign dignitaries on official visits to Spain.
The gardens in front of the palace are open to the public during
the opening times of the palace; both are closed if there is an
official guest in residence.

The gardens now consist of several areas. There is a formal
semicircular area in front of the palace where mopheaded *Catalpa
bignonoides* mark time as if on a parade ground. Closely clipped
box in mound shapes keep them company. Along the ceremonial
driveway lawns dotted with splashes of colourful bedding dazzle
in the heat of the day. A calmer atmosphere exists in the garden
areas to the left and right of the roadway. Here mature specimens
of Wellingtonia (*Sequoiadendron giganteum*) and cedars rise and
spread from the bounds of well-maintained box hedging.

The palace moat was converted into a garden in Felipe II's
reign (1556–98) and according to contemporary accounts it was
a fragrant, floriferous garden resonant with the sounds of more
exotic birds. Still grassed and the walls creeper-clad, its only
claim to flowers is from cherry trees and other fruit trees.

Mature trees and statuary in a
courtyard garden near the main
entrance to the palace.

22 *Toledo: El Cigarral de Menores*

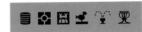

open: By appointment

Location: Carretera de Piedrabuena 68, 45004 Toledo

There are a few surviving properties called *cigarrales*. The name refers to the noise made by crickets on hot summer nights, and is also a collective name for small country houses or farms that generally were lived in by minor clergy, especially those resting or recuperating from ill health. The *cigarrales* of Toledo are all found on the opposite banks of the River Tajo (Tagus) to the city of Toledo. Their gardens have a particular vernacular because of the steep terrain and the horticulture of their former occupants. El Cigarral de Menores has been in the ownership of the Marañón family since the Toledan writer Dr Gregorio Marañón bought it in 1922.

Dating from 1617, it has a paved entrance area where sentinel cypresses stand guard at the door. Little beds are edged with box and myrtle hedging and although a relatively small garden, there is space for fountains, a pool, and a glasshouse.

Part of the charm of this garden is the integration of the various levels with the surrounding olive groves and orchards, as much as with the city of Toledo. There are some important modern pieces of statuary including *Lugar de Asiento* (*A Sitting Place*) by Eduardo Chillida, which was installed in 1986 to commemorate the centenary of the birth of the late Dr Marañón.

Further information from:
Señor Gregorio Marañón y
Bertran de Lis
Tel: 91 521 82 19 (Madrid)

Nearby sights of interest:
The city of Toledo.

Small beds edged with box or myrtle.

23 *Valencia: Jardín Botánico de Valencia*

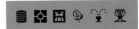

open: Tue to Sun, summer 10am–9pm and winter 10am–6pm; closes 25 Dec and 1 Jan; students, pensioners, and children under ten years free entry

Location: Calle Beato de Gaspar de Bono 6, in the NW of the city

Valencia's botanic garden was founded in 1651 and relocated to this site in 1802. It is arranged like many early gardens of this sort, on a grid system of rectangular beds for different plant groups. Palms, water plants, alpines, and native Valencian plants are well represented. Other groupings include medicinal plants, plants of economic importance, ornamentals, succulents, and cacti. At the centre of the garden are several large glasshouses and a shadehouse, or *umbraculum*, built in 1897 by Arturo Mélida. The tropical glasshouse, 465 sq m (5,003 sq ft) of glass made up from 4,342 individual panes, is one of the most important buildings in the history of iron architecture in Spain. It was built between 1860 and 1862 under the direction of Sebastián Monleón.

Further information from:
Jardín Botánico de Valencia,
Universidad de Valencia, Beato
Gaspar de Bono 6, 46008 Valencia
Tel: 96 391 16 57

Nearby sights of interest:
Museo San Pío V; Jardines del Río Turia (see p.65); El Jardín de Monforte (see p.64); Torres de Serranos; La Lonja.

open: Daily, 21 Mar to
20 Sep 10.30am–8pm and 21 Sep
to 20 Mar 10.30am–6pm

Further information from:
Fundación Pública Municipal de
Parques y Jardines Singulares,
Ajuntament de Valencia
Tel: 96 352 54 78

Nearby sights of interest:
Museo San Pío V; Jardines del
Río Turia (see p.65); Torres de
Serranos; La Lonja.

Lions guard the entrance.

24 Valencia: El Jardín de Monforte

Location: Calle Monforte 5, Valencia

Completed in 1859 Monforte is a formal garden in the romantic neoclassical style of the 19th century. The garden was designed and built by the Valencian architect Sebastián Monleón. In 1941 it was declared an "Artistic Garden", assuring its future preservation. Like so many surviving romantic gardens it is no longer a place set apart and urban development is all around it.

Nonetheless it is still an atmospheric and important garden with a lake, grotto, parterres and closely clipped box, myrtle, and cypress. Stairways, statuary and paths have been preserved, and it has an intimate harmonious feel to it. In summer the fragrance of citrus flowers hangs in the air. Most of the statuary is of carrara marble. Of special importance are the two lions, which guard the garden's entrance, made of the white stone quarried near Colmenar in Castilla-La Mancha and sculpted in Madrid by José Bellver in 1860.

In summer welcome shade is offered by the dramatic iron pergola holding an ancient and vanilla-scented wisteria. Although the collection of plants is not necessarily rare, they reflect the introductions and plant fashions of successive eras and among them are cypress, *Erythrina crista-galli*, *Magnolia grandiflora*, and *Gingko biloba*. Flowering plants include many bulbous specimens such as amaryllis, dahlia, freesia, hyacinth, narcissus, and tulip. Bear's breeches (*Acanthus mollis*) is much favoured in the planting under trees.

open: All year, daily, 8am
to sunset

Further information from:
Fundación Pública Municipal de
Parques y Jardines Singulares,
Ajuntament de Valencia
Tel: 96 352 54 78

Nearby sights of interest:
Museo San Pío V; Jardines del
Río Turia (see p.65); Torres de
Serranos; La Lonja.

25 Valencia: Jardines del Real

Location: Calle San Pío V, Valencia

Jardines del Real was once the garden surrounding the Palacio Real, but over the years has evolved into one of the city's public parks. It was opened to the public in 1823 as the Jardines la Cátedra de Botánica de la Universidad de Valencia. In 1902 the municipal nursery was installed, hence its local name as Los Viveros (nursery).

Statuary and layout are reminiscent of its past splendour but it is a modern park with good facilities including ponds, recreational areas, and a small zoo. One of the more interesting features is a formal rose garden with closely clipped, shaped trees and low hedging.

26 *Valencia: Jardines del Río Turia*

Location: The bed of the River Turia, Valencia

A 5km (3 mile) stretch of the River Turia which used to flood disastrously has been transformed into a park. Work began in the late 1980s when the course of the river was diverted. The resulting park is maturing well and consists of lawns, avenues of trees, and shrub plantings.

Laid out along the former river bed are also playing fields and children's playgrounds. The star attraction for children is a larger-than-life-size figure of Gulliver, pegged to the ground and accessible by steps and slides. Within the figure is a model of the city of Valencia. The river bed is still crossed by numerous bridges.

open: All year, daily, dawn to dusk

Further information from:
Fundación Pública Municipal de Parques y Jardines Singulares, Ajuntament de Valencia
Tel: 96 352 54 78

Nearby sights of interest:
Jardines del Real (Viveros) (see opposite); Instituto Valenciano de Arte Moderno; Torres de Serranos.

The river bed was transformed by urban landscaping.

Key to gardens

1 Jardines del Alcázar
  de los Reyes Cristianos
2 Jardín Botánico de Córdoba
3 Madinat al-Zahra
4 Patio de los Naranjos
5 Palacio de Viana
6 Carmen de Rodríguez-Acosta
7 Alhambra and Generalife

8 Casa Museo Manuel de Falla
9 Parque García Lorca
10 Carmen de los Mártires
11 Bodega Gardens
12 La Concepción
13 Paseo del Parque
14 El Retiro
15 Museo de Bonsai

16 Jardines de los Reales
  Alcázares
17 La Cartuja
18 Parque de María Luisa
19 Patio do los Naranjos
20 Casa de Pilatos
21 Hospital de los Venerables
  Sacerdotes

Key

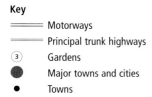

═══ Motorways
═══ Principal trunk highways
③ Gardens
● Major towns and cities
• Towns

Southern Spain

The southern region of Spain, although made up of many provinces, is collectively known as Andalucía. It is bordered on the north by a range of mountains, the Sierra Morena, on the west by the Atlantic, and to the south by the Mediterranean. It has hot dry summers and generally mild winters, but there are variations due to the mountainous nature of the inland areas. Both Seville and Cordoba, however, can experience high summer temperatures up to 45°C (113°F). Annual rainfall is variable and in recent years there have been wet autumns, followed by seriously dry winters. Despite the dryness of the region it is very much Spain's garden with vineyards producing wine in several provinces, tropical fruits grown outdoors, and strawberries from Huelva and Malaga. Olives and citrus are also grown in large-scale groves in various parts of southern Spain. The reason for such abundance is due to the centuries old irrigation which was begun by the Romans and perfected by the Moors, who also introduced palms and crops including oranges and sugar to the area.

In Cordoba, where the Western Umayyad Caliphate dynasty was established in the 8th century, there was an outstanding garden at Madinat al-Zahra, now an excavated site.

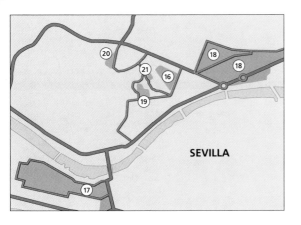

Battlements shaped in cypress enclose areas of the Generalife gardens, Granada.

The entrance patio at the Palacio de Viana, Cordoba, sets the scene for the patios to follow.

By the 10th century Cordoba had become a centre of botanical knowledge but it has only recently had its own botanic garden, which holds an extensive collection of olives, among other economic plants.

Seville and Granada were centres of horticulture under the Moorish rulers. When the reconquest of Granada finally occurred in the late 15th century many of the greatest Moorish sourcebooks were destroyed, among them the *Treatise of Agriculture* by Ibn Luyun. Fortunately translations have survived and from them we can discover many of the plants that were grown as ornamentals, as well as economic crops, in Spanish gardens prior to the 15th century. Among them were citrus, jasmine, myrtle, and palms. Iris, Madonna lily, morning glory, fragrant stocks, and waterlilies are some of the plants that were listed for the first time between the 10th and 11th centuries.

Further waves of plants arrived in Spain in the 16th century as a result of Spanish explorations in the New World. Many of them came into Europe from Seville, where there were several scholars who played a part in maintaining gardens to acclimatize these new plants. One of them was the physician Nicolás Monardes (there is a plaque honouring him in Calle Sierpes, where his garden once was in Seville). These early initiatives were echoed in the 20th century when the Universal Exhibition (Expo 92) was held in Seville to commemorate the discovery of America. Once again new species were sent to Spain from Ibero-American countries and it is hoped that many of them will become popular in Spanish gardens.

Citrus, lavender, and rosemary perfume the beds around the inner pool of the Alcázar, Cordoba.

Leaves cascade down a small, shell-encrusted water ladder at Malaga's El Retiro park.

In late spring and early summer southern cities such as Granada and Cordoba overflow with flower-covered walls, and window boxes and patios are filled with brightly coloured flowering plants. May is the month to enjoy Cordoba's patio festival.

Apart from the patios and the historical gardens of Moorish Spain, there are many new gardens that will in time mature and become popular destinations. The arboretum at Carambola is situated over one of Seville's reservoirs. Once its trees and shrubs are mature there will be double the reason to put it on the map.

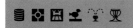

open: Summer, Mon to Sat 10am–2pm and 6–8pm, Sun and Public Holidays 9.30am–4pm; winter, Mon to Sat 10am–2pm and 4.30–6.30pm, Sun and Public Holidays 9.30am–3pm

open: As above

Further information from:
Oficina Municipal de Información Turística, Plaza Judá Leví,
14003 Córdoba
Tel: 957 20 05 22

Nearby sights of interest:
Mezquita-Catedral; Alcázar de los Reyes Cristianos; Palacio de Viana (see p.72); Jardín Botánico de Córdoba (see below); Patio de los Naranjos (see p.72).

Córdoba: Jardines del Alcázar de los Reyes Cristianos

Location: In the grounds of the Alcázar

The Alcázar dates from 1328 when it was built for Alfonso XI. The Christian Monarchs, Fernando and Isabel, stayed in the palace during their campaign to regain Granada from the Moors. In the 1950s its gardens were restored and opened to visitors.

A walk through the Alcázar interior reveals one of the many limpid and evocative indoor patios in southern Spain. Loquats, citrus, myrtle, and other herbs fill a formal parterre area near the baths. Once you step outside the building into the fortified grounds the sense of space is overwhelming. The extensive gardens in the style of their 15th-century Moorish origins are on several levels and dominated by carp pools and water features, and an avenue of large, closely clipped cypresses. Oranges, pruned into rounded shapes, and roses provide the main structure.

---

open: Tue to Sun, summer 10.30am–2.30pm and 5.30–7.30pm, winter 10.30am–2.30pm and 4.30–6.30pm; closes mid-Jul to mid-Sep

open: As above

Further information from:
Jardín Botánico de Córdoba, Avenida Linneo, s/n, 14004 Córdoba
Tel: 957 20 00 18

This large greenhouse holds a collection of American flora.

Córdoba: Jardín Botánico de Córdoba

Location: SW of the city centre on the right bank of the River Guadalquivir

Jardín Botánico de Córdoba is among Spain's more recent botanic gardens and was officially inaugurated in 1987.

The site is divided into several areas and it takes about two hours to walk around its entirety. It fulfils the usual research roles of a botanic garden, but the layout here is different from most botanic institutions. Well-shaped citrus hedges enclose the order beds, transforming them into family rooms and perfuming the air with orange blossom in spring. The beds are lined with low-growing rosemary and dwarf pomegranate hedges. All through the gardens shade trees offer respite from the heat of the sun.

Of particular interest are the collections of economic, food, industrial, and medicinal plants held as the Agricultural School. A garden for the blind holds a range of aromatic, as well as textured-foliage plants. The arboretum consists of deciduous and evergreen plants, palms, conifers, and shrubs.

The exhibition greenhouse holds one of the most complete collections of endemic Canarian flora in Spain. There is an attractive rose garden laid out around an octagonal fountain.

Córdoba: Madinat al-Zahra

Location: On the slopes of the Sierra Morena, 8km (5 miles) W of Cordoba off the C431

Madinat al-Zahra's gardens evoke the splendours of the past beauty of the palace built here in the 10th century by the Caliph Abd al-Rahman. The gardens are set in the foundations and ruins of what was to be a city of great importance, where the Caliph would establish his Caliphate. The statistics noting manpower and materials are staggering, and the lavishness and beauty of the site overwhelmed those who visited at its inception. However it was an ephemeral beauty that lasted no more than 75 years, when it was destroyed by warfare. Referred to as Vieja Córdoba (Old Cordoba) the ruins lay undisturbed until 1922 when excavation began on the site. The city's buildings and roads have been restored as far as possible, given the looting of much of the material over the years.

The site's original garden consisted of pools, canals, and fountains, and included a dazzling basin filled with quicksilver. Today, within the partially excavated foundations, once formal plantings have matured into free-flowing shapes. Pencil-thin cypresses rise skyward making dark outlines against the canvas of the open landscape. Oleanders, strawberry tree (*Arbutus unedo*), and pomegranates make stylish accents, while bougainvilleas hang in swathes across archways and walls. Palms add images of a more desert-like landscape and in spring the site is full of wildflowers.

open: 1 May to 30 Sep, Tue to Sat, 10am–2pm and 6–8.30pm; 1 Oct to 30 Apr, Tue to Sat, 10am–2pm and 4–6.30pm; Sun and Public Holidays (closes Mon), 10am–2pm

Further information from:
Madinat al-Zahra, Carretera de Palma del Río, Km 8, Córdoba
Tel: 957 32 91 30

Nearby sights of interest:
Mezquita-Catedral; Jardines del Alcázar de los Reyes Cristianos (see p.70); Jardín Botánico de Córdoba (see p.70); Patio de los Naranjos (see p.72); Callejón de los Flores; Palacio de Viana (see p.72); Castillo del Almodóvar del Río.

Palms rise out of the excavated ruins of the once-powerful site of old Cordoba.

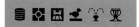

open: Daily, summer
10am–7pm, winter 10am–5.30pm

Further information from:
Mezquita-Catedral, Calle Torrijos,
10, Córdoba
Tel: 957 47 05 12

Nearby sights of interest:
Jardines del Alcázar de los Reyes
Cristianos (see p.70).

Orange trees in the patio.

4 *Córdoba: Patio de los Naranjos*

Location: In the courtyard of the Mezquita-Catedral de Córdoba

The Orange Tree Patio or Court on the northern side of Cordoba's extraordinary mosque-cathedral is on a site that has been continuously gardened since the 8th century, when the mosque was built. The courtyard first held palm trees, then it was extended and records show that orange trees were grown here from the 15th century onwards. In the 18th century olives and cypresses also grew here. Arranged in symmetrical ranks of rigid straight lines, the clipped mopheads of the trees and their glowing fruits soften the plain rectangular layout.

At the feet of the trees in straight lines across the cobbled courtyard run row upon row of irrigation channels. There are several fountains and pools, and underneath the patio is a huge water tank which provided water for Muslim cleansing rites.

The straight stark trunks of the orange trees are a fitting outdoor prelude to the forest of columns and arches that are among the awe-inspiring treasures in the mosque-cathedral.

---

open: 1 Oct to 1 Jun, daily
except Wed, 10am–1pm and
4–6pm and Sun and Public
Holidays 10am–2pm; 16 Jun to
30 Sep, daily, 10am–2pm; closes
1 to 15 Jun except for patios; free
entry Tue
open: As above

Further information from:
Palacio Museo de Viana, Obra
Cultural de la Caja Provincial
de Ahorros de Córdoba, Plaza
de Don Gome, 2, Córdoba
Tel: 957 48 01 34

Nearby sights of interest:
Mezquita-Catedral; Jardines del
Alcázar de los Reyes Cristianos
(see p.70); Jardín Botánico de
Córdoba (see p.70); Patio de los
Naranjos (see above); Callejón
de las Flores.

5 *Córdoba: Palacio de Viana*

Location: N of the city centre on Plaza de Don Gome, 2

Dating from the 17th century, the Palacio de Viana was sold to a Provincial Bank in 1980. After restoration the building and its 13 or 14 patios were opened to the public. The mansion and garden provide a "snapshot in time" of family life. Visits to the garden are unaccompanied, but tours of the house are guided. Each patio is well marked and has its own character determined by the planting and its shape.

Climbing plants, such as plumbago and bougainvillea, clothe the walls, while formal shape is offered in some of the patios by clipped box hedges. At the heart of the outdoor area is the Palace Garden, a large rectangle divided into numerous smaller formal sections. Roses, oleander, citrus, and lilies perfume the air in their turn. At its centre is an ancient holm oak, taller even than the palms that grow in this part of the garden.

Depending on the timing of your visit, some patios will be in deep and cooling shade and others in bright, almost blinding, sunlight. Water plays in pools and fountains to cool and calm the heat, and all through the patios there are seasonal collections of herbs and flowering plants.

Granada: Carmen de Rodríguez-Acosta

Location: On the hillside below the Alhambra

Built between 1914 and 1928 the white, geometric-style *carmen* of the painter Jose-Maria Rodríguez-Acosta is now a museum. White retaining walls follow the slope and terraces of the land in great steps. Although 20th century in its style, the terraced garden seems almost biblical. Italian cypresses sky-rocketing heavenwards in groups fill the corners of the terraces, while others are clipped into architectural shapes. These strong forms echo the lines of the house and walls, and make such emphatic statements that the absence of flowers is hardly noticeable. Geraniums and roses offer colour in this evocative garden, the perfect setting for the collection of classical statuary.

open: By appointment (can be arranged from one day to the next)
open: As above

Further information from:
Museo Gomez Moreno-Fundación Rodríguez-Acosta, Callejón Niño del Rollo 8, Granada
Tel: 958 22 74 97

Nearby sights of interest:
Alhambra and Generalife (see pp.74–7); Carmen de los Mártires (see p.79); El Bañuelo (brick-vaulted Arab baths).

Built between 1914 and 1928, the painter's villa garden holds an evocative combination of plants and statuary.

open: Daily, summer
9am–8pm and winter 9am–6pm;
last admissions 15 minutes
before closing
open: As above

Further information from:
Tourist Office, Corral del Carbón,
Mariana Pineda, 18001 Granada
Tel: 958 22 59 90
or Alhambra and Generalife offices
Tel: 958 22 75 27

Nearby sights of interest:
Carmen de los Mártires (see p.79).

Granada: Alhambra and Generalife

Location: E of the city centre

The Alhambra is high on the list of every visitor to Granada for
its overall drama and beauty. But for the garden visitor there is an
additional richness in the wooded landscape around the citadel,
as well as in the patios and open spaces within the buildings.

Each patio or court plays a deep and important part in the life
and meaning of the Alhambra buildings; stepping into the light
and openness of one of the patios marks a dramatic change from
the shady, highly ornate interiors. But these exterior spaces are
controlled and geometric, with water, sky, reflections, and
sound playing an equal part. Meditation and ablution
may have been their origins; today
they can play the same role
albeit metaphorically

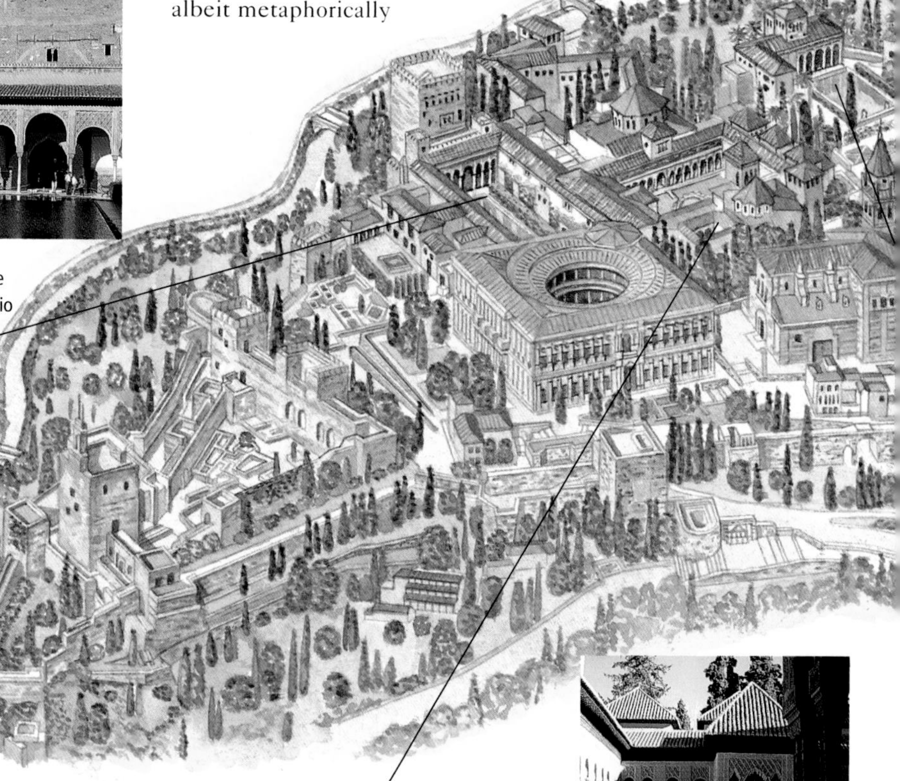

Clipped myrtles line
two sides of the Patio
de los Arrayanes.

A fountain supported
by twelve stone lions
lies at the centre of the
Patio de los Leones.

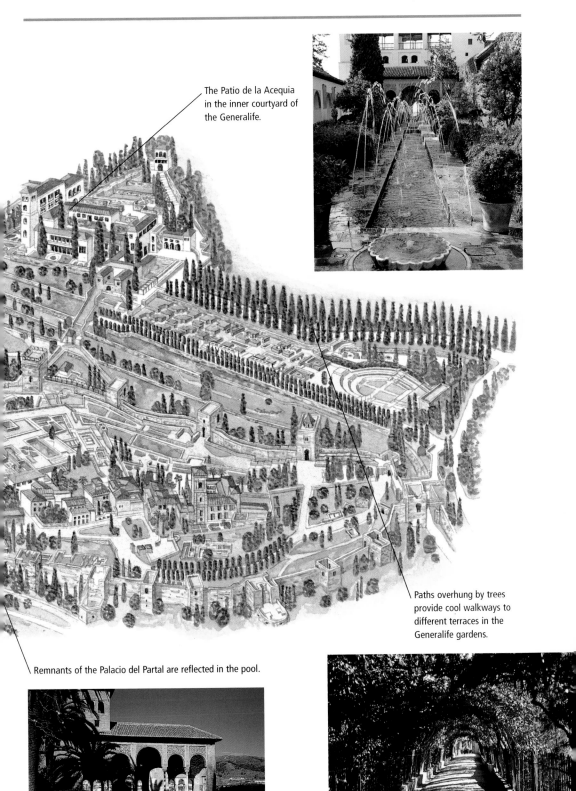

The Patio de la Acequia in the inner courtyard of the Generalife.

Paths overhung by trees provide cool walkways to different terraces in the Generalife gardens.

Remnants of the Palacio del Partal are reflected in the pool.

Roses trained on iron arches provide colour and fragrance as well as shade in the Generalife gardens.

The view from the Generalife gardens across to the wall and battlements of the Alhambra.

cleansing, but it is difficult to experience the patios as they should be due to the crowds of visitors. Within the Royal Palace there are several major courtyards which you will come to as you progress through the building. The first of these, the Patio de los Arrayanes (Myrtles) or Patio de la Alberca (Pool), was the creation of the Moorish ruler Yusuf I and dates from the 14th century. It is the absence of elaborate ornament and the starkness of the pool's line and its surrounding courtyard that make the impact. The planting of well-clipped hedges of myrtle reinforces the simplicity of the patio. The myrtle hedges were put in place in the 19th century and there are no full records of what the original planting consisted of, but some visitors in the 16th century noted citrus trees. Additional ambience comes at different times of day when the sunlight seems to colour the façades, and the still water of the pool reflects the arches and colonnades of the surrounding buildings.

The second courtyard, the Patio de los Leones (Patio of the Lions), was built by Yusuf's son Muhammad V later in the 14th century. It is an embodiment of the Persian pleasure garden. The scheme of an enclosed space divided by four channels, or watercourses, representing the holy rivers of Persia was seen by nomadic Arabs as the paradise gardens of the Koran. In this patio the central feature is a stone basin supported by a hexagonal base, surrounded by twelve carved lions. Water flows along the

channels and thin jets of water spill from the lions' mouths. At one time the quadrants, which in Persian pleasure gardens represented earth, air, water, and fire, were much lower than the water channels. In this patio the play of light and shade, and the harmony of central space with the surrounding façades, is as dramatic as that of the Patio de los Arrayanes.

Outside the Palacio de los Leones are the remnants of another palace, the Partal. Here exposed to the elements is the *alberca*, or pool. Unenclosed by buildings it offers a different type of beauty. Rising from the Partal there are many terraces, each holding foundations of buildings. Within them now are gardens with pools, hedges, and shrubs. They date from 1924 and are the work of the architects responsible for the overall restoration at the Alhambra, Modesto Cendoya and Leopoldo Torres Balbás. There is an elemental quality in their plantings, with cypresses and poplar making a strong framework.

In the Alcazaba ruins to the west of the palaces there are stunning views over Granada, towards the snow-capped Sierra Nevada and to the adjacent hills where you can glimpse some of the present *carmen* or villa gardens.

The Generalife gardens are the oldest in Granada and date from the early 14th century. The palace and its gardens were meant as a summer retreat for the Sultans. The hillside was terraced and water channels laid in. Here vegetables and herbs were grown, and although the terracing remains and the area is still used for growing vegetables it has lost much of its original productivity. The gardens nearer the palace are the work of Francisco Prieto Moreno and date from the 1950s. His designs hold many elements of what might once have been on the site. In the main it consists of parterres and hedged garden rooms, many with pools and fountains.

The most famous water garden is here in the palace. Known as the Patio de la Acequia (Court of the Long Pond), its main feature is a long narrow channel of water with thin jets of water that hop in arches across from side to side. Brightly coloured flowers tumble from nearby pots. Above this part of the palace is a doorway through to the Patio de los Cipreses (Court of the Cypresses), where square islands of oleander float in water channels and jets of water dance from bed to bed. Higher up the hillside is the Moorish Escalera del Agua, a staircase where water flows down what is in effect a stone banister. Dominating the landscape around these gardens are the pencil-like Italian cypresses of the shady Paseo de los Cipreses (Promenade of Cypresses), and the tunnels of oleander.

The snow-capped Sierra Nevada mountains dominate views around the Alhambra.

Water fountains of different shapes and styles provide welcome respite from the heat.

open: Tue to Sat, Apr to Sep 9am–3pm and Oct to Mar 10am–4pm

open: As above

Further information from:
Casa Museo Manuel de Falla,
Calle Antequeruela Alta, 11,
Granada
Tel: 958 22 94 21

Nearby sights of interest:
Alhambra and Generalife
(see pp.74–7); Carmen de
los Mártires (see opposite);
El Bañuelo (brick-vaulted
Arab baths).

8 *Granada: Casa Museo Manuel de Falla*

Location: SW of the Alhambra on Calle Antequeruela Alta

The entrance to the small but very evocative garden is through the main house, which is now a museum dedicated to the life and work of the Spanish composer, Manuel de Falla (1876–1946). The garden is really a terrace adjoining the house, with a view of Granada and the Alhambra. The front wall of the terrace is lined with terracotta pots filled with geraniums and supports a mass of sweet-smelling honeysuckle. Box-edged beds with roses and cypresses are the main formal element of the garden.

Like all Granadan gardens water plays a major part. Here it has its source in an interesting plant-covered fountain. Water seems to trickle out of nowhere into a large terracotta urn, making a gentle sound and creating a small play of light and movement in the shade of the plants.

open: All year, daily, 8am–10pm

open: Tue to Sun, 10am–1pm and 5–8pm; admission charge except Sun and Public Holidays

Further information from:
Casa Museo Garcia Lorca,
Calle Arabial, Granada
Tel: 958 25 84 66

Nearby sights of interest:
Catedral; Corral del Carbón.

Roses at Parque García Lorca.

9 *Granada: Parque García Lorca (also called Huerta de San Vincente)*

Location: W of the city centre on Calle Arabial

The Huerta de San Vincente was once a fruit orchard where Granada's celebrated poet García Lorca spent family summer holidays. Their summer home has now been restored and is a museum holding furniture, posters, and other artefacts. It has its own separate opening times and does have an admission charge.

The park has been transformed into a huge rose garden, probably one of Europe's largest, complete with formal pools and fountains. Even so, with the proximity of the city centre it is hard to reconcile this as the place Lorca described as "A paradise of trees and water and so much jasmine . . .".

All the roses are well labelled and some of them are grown in box-edged beds, but most, including *Rosa* 'Susan Hampshire', *R*. 'Sonia Meilland', *R*. 'Super Star', and *R*. 'Ballerina', are in rectangular beds. Height is offered by cypresses cut into pyramid shapes. Aromatic pleasures, apart from the roses, are on offer from numerous tapestry-like plantings of lavender and cotton lavender. There is a row of gnarled old olive trees, probably remnants of the original orchard garden.

Granada: Carmen de los Mártires

Location: W of the Alhambra on Paseo de los Mártires

Within walking distance of the Alhambra, the 19th-century villa and garden of Carmen de los Mártires have recently been restored. As you enter the grounds the first view is of a ferny grotto complete with water nymph and royal visitor plaques, framed by two huge palms.

Made up of terraces on different levels, some enclosed with walls of clipped cypresses and others more open, the garden is a leafy, shady haven with a view south-west over the city. Palm tree fronds and citrus trees frame the picture. On one side of the villa are several terraces not open to the public, but on the other is a grove of palms with a formal three-tiered fountain in the middle of the box-edged beds. Arum lilies flourish in the rim of the pool. Water plays an important role in the courtyard canal, where a grotto and Moorish-style walls are in place. It is reached through an entrance off the main terrace, which holds palms, citrus trees, and roses within box-edged borders. There is ample statuary and a large circular pool at its centre.

open: All year, Mon to Fri, 10am–2pm and 5–7pm; closes Public Holidays

Further information from:
Carmen de los Mártires, Paseo de los Mártires, Granada
Tel: 958 22 79 53

Nearby sights of interest:
Alhambra and Generalife (see pp.74–7); El Bañuelo (brick-vaulted Arab baths); Casa Museo Manuel de Falla (see opposite).

Arum lilies flourish in the pool at the base of the dramatic three-tiered fountain in a palm grove behind the house.

Jerez: Bodega Gardens

Location: Various locations in and around Jerez

open: Check times with individual *bodegas*

Further information from:
Individual Sherry Houses or Informacíon Turística, Plaza Estévez, s/n, Jerez
Tel: 928 69 66 55

Nearby sights of interest:
Alameda Vieja and Alcázar; Parque Zoológico.

Box-edged beds at González Byass.

Tasting sherry and touring the sun-drenched white-washed sherry houses of Jerez is a delightful pastime. Many of the *bodegas* were established in the 18th century and were formed around palatial manor houses. Today, the business part of each enterprise is highly commercial and uses modern production techniques. In most cases, however, the original gardens are still in place with their mature conifer and palm plantings.

At the Jardines de Domecq, Norfolk Island pine, umbrella pine, and Monterey and Arizona cypresses rise above the sweeping lawns. Numerous palms, including Canary island date palm (*Phoenix canariensis*) and the sabal palm, are grown for their trunks, foliage, and fruit, while many flowering shrubs, climbers, and evergreens offer a colourful framework.

At González Byass there are parterres and several architectural features worth investigating. The large circular above-ground cellar, La Concha, a confection of iron and opaque glass, is the work of the French engineer Eiffel (the architect of the Eiffel Tower). He also built a delightful arbour structure in iron.

Williams and Humbert near the bull ring of Jerez have a more traditional garden, laid mainly to lawn with an avenue of palms, clouds of bougainvillea, and flowering shrubs. After bullfights tradition holds that most of the audience repair to the *bodega* for a fortifying and refreshing tipple.

Málaga: La Concepción

Location: About 7km (4¼ miles) N of Malaga, on the N331 towards Antequera take a signed exit on the right and cross under the motorway

open: Tue to Sun; spring 10am–8pm, summer 10am–9pm, autumn 10am–7pm, winter 10am–5.30pm; closes 25 Dec, 1 Jan; check time of last admission

Further information from:
Jardín Botánico-Histórico La Concepción, Carretera de Las Pedrizas (CN331) Km 166, 29014 Málaga
Tel: 952 25 21 48
Fax: 952 25 74 42

Nearby sights of interest:
El Retiro (see p.82); Paseo del Parque (see opposite); Museo de Bonsai (see p.82).

The gardens at La Concepción were begun in 1889 as private pleasure grounds attached to the house of Thomas Livermore, British consul in Malaga. The house and garden were sold to the municipality of Malaga and the gardens opened to the public in 1994. In the special microclimate here interest in plants has resulted in a tropical, yet Mediterranean paradise garden. The Swiss cheese plant (*Monstera deliciosa*) acts as an exotic ground-covering plant, with its shiny leathery leaves glistening near pools and waterfalls. Bamboo groves, stands of *Alpinia zerumbet*, and huge specimens of *Ficus microcarpa* are among the plants that flourish here. Two species of strelitzia, the giant *Strelitzia nicolai* and the small and brightly coloured *S. reginae*, or bird of paradise, make strong architectural statements. Hibiscus and clivias are among other flowering plants, but in late March it is scent that makes a powerful impact. Much of the garden is perfumed by the fragrance of Japanese mock orange (*Pittosporum tobira*), and near the elegant Georgian house wisteria and jasmine leap from their stately iron pergola to sweep through the mature trees, palms and pines among them.

Visitors are taken around the garden in groups of varying sizes, led by knowledgeable guides. The visit follows a route along sandy paths lined with stone irrigation gulleys and past many water features, including a waterfall, pools, and up an avenue lined with palms. The avenue leads eventually to a viewpoint, where from a classical gazebo you gaze across the humming motorway to the urban sprawl of Malaga.

Málaga: Paseo del Parque

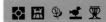

Location: Near the port to the eastern side of Malaga

open: At all times

The Paseo del Parque is a perfect place to see the most Spanish of activities, the *paseo* or evening stroll, take place around dusk each day. The park is on both sides of the main east–west road through Malaga which starts as the Avenida de Andalucía, becomes the Alameda Principal, and leads in to the Paseo del Parque.

The park was laid out at the turn of the century on land reclaimed when the Cánovas Harbour was built. Sculpture including Pimentel's *El Cenachero* (*The Fishmonger*) and *El Jazminero* (*The Jasmine-seller*) is mostly situated in the various shady, enclosed sitting places or *glorietas*. The original plantings of palms and flowering trees give the park an elegant and established atmosphere.

Buildings on the Paseo include the Art Nouveau town hall, the Ayuntamiento, but it is the lush exuberance of the palms, conifers, and flowering trees and shrubs that stay in the memory. *Strelitzia nicolai*, the tall-growing bird of paradise, cycads, and huge bamboos all provide contrasting foliage and shapes, while colour comes from dense plantings of orange clivias, white arum lilies, jacaranda, brunsfelsia, and *Chorisia speciosa*. Striking foliage contrasts are made by many plants, including hedges of *Acalypha wilkesiana* and the elephantine leaves of alocasia.

Balloon-sellers, roller-bladers, children in prams and on foot, as well as families, mingle happily in the exciting atmosphere of Malaga's Paseo del Parque.

Further information from:
Turismo, Pasaje de Chinitas 4, Málaga
Tel: 952 21 34 45

Nearby sights of interest:
Alcazaba; Museo Arqueológico; Casa Natal de Picasso; Catedral; Museo de Bellas Artes.

Statuary in a shady *glorieta*.

open: Daily, spring 9am–8pm (last entry 7pm) and winter 9am–6pm (last entry 5pm)

Further information from:
El Retiro, Ecoparque SA,
Carretera de Coin s/n,
29140 Churriana, Málaga
Tel: 952 62 16 00
Fax: 952 62 26 54

Nearby sights of interest:
Paseo del Parque (see p.81);
La Concepción (see pp.80–1);
Refugio Juanar; Museo de Bonsai
(see below).

Among the plants in Siren's garden are an avocado, sago palms, and a queen palm.

14 *Málaga: El Retiro*

Location: 12km (7½ miles) SW of Malaga on the C344 near Alhaurín de la Torre

Like many of Spain's so-called "Artistic Gardens", El Retiro has suffered much neglect in the past. Now much visited, this romantic garden shares the site with an ornithological park. Despite this, there is still delight in strolling through a garden that combines Italianate influences with astonishing views over Malaga.

The house and garden were established in the 17th century as the retreat of the Bishop of Malaga, Alonso de Santo Tomás, thought to be an illegitimate son of Filipe IV. The property eventually passed into the hands of the Count of Villalcázar de Sirga, a patron of art and literature, who enlarged the buildings and created new gardens.

The one remaining feature of the Bishop's 17th-century garden is a covered walkway, quite overgrown with vines. It forms a cross and at the meeting point of four paths there is a sunken fountain, reminiscent of that at the Hospital de los Venerables Sacerdotes (see p.87).

Villalcázar's additions included orchards, remnants of which consist of a patio and pleasure gardens complete with statuary and fountains. Two of these areas, the Jardín de la Sirena and the Cascade, were completed by the end of the 18th century. The Cascade is a wonderful descent of water moving through three levels. Statuary symbolizing rivers spill water from vases.

The overall atmosphere is slightly muddled because of the dual identity of the garden, but once you are in the water garden, or even walking through the orchards, it is easy to imagine the garden's early life as a romantic pleasure ground.

---

open: All year, daily, 10am–1.30pm and 4–7pm

Further information from:
Museo de Bonsai, Parque Arroyo
de la Represa, Avenida del Dr
Maiz Viñal, Marbella
Tel: 95 286 29 26

Nearby sights of interest:
Costa del Sol; Mijas; Puerto
Banús; Refugio Juanar.

15 *Marbella: Museo de Bonsai*

Location: In the Parque Arroyo de la Represa, Marbella

Set in the midst of a well-used new park that follows the course of an old river, the Museo de Bonsai is a meditative, calming, and cooling place. Shaded rooms with display benches carry old, gnarled but miniature specimens of flora from many regions. The owner of the museum, Miguel Angel Garcia, has grouped the bonsai plants into naturalistic locations but many of them are too large (even for bonsai) to fit into a realistic grouping. This museum is thought to be the first and possibly only private collection in Spain open to the public. Here you can see the fascinating characteristics trees and shrubs manifest on the small scale.

Sevilla: Jardines de los Reales Alcázares

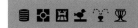

Location: SE of the cathedral on the Plaza del Triunfo

The building of the Royal Fortress began in the 10th century and successive rulers and monarchs have added to it over the years. Similarly its extensive gardens have grown and developed over time. Taking up nearly 16ha (40 acres) the gardens started out as Moorish "gardens of delights", but the only remnant of this era is a wall dividing the orchards from domestic gardens. The gardens were largely rebuilt under the Christian monarchy beginning with Pedro the Cruel in 1366. Many Islamic elements of water, fountains, tilework, and enclosures were provided by the Mudéjar workmen employed by him, but the style that predominates is of the 18th or 19th century.

In all there are 18 named garden areas to explore. You can walk out of the palace into several of the patios. Near the palace they are enclosed and the fragrance of orange blossom and jasmine are held closely within them. The highest, in terms of the level of the land, is the Garden of Mercury's Pool. The rectangular pool has a bronze statue and fountain representing Mercury at its centre.

As the gardens move away from the palace they become larger and, although still enclosed and discrete, they seem more relaxed in style and plantings, until you reach the English Garden, laid out like a landscape park.

Wherever you walk in the vast expanses of the Alcázares gardens there are places to sit and enjoy the birdsong and shade. Particularly lovely are the poolside seats in the Poet's Garden. Here cypress trees make a dramatic enclosure for the rectangular pools of the area.

Palm trees, bitter oranges, *Magnolia grandiflora*, peaches, roses, and almonds, as well as fragrant *Pittosporum tobira*, are among the plants that luxuriate in this "paradise" garden in one of Spain's busiest and most crowded cities.

open: All year, Tue to Sat 9.30am–4pm and Sun 10am–1pm
open: As above

Further information from:
Reales Alcázares, Plaza del Triunfo, Sevilla
Tel: 95 422 71 63

Nearby sights of interest:
Hospital de los Venerables Sacerdotes (see p.87); Plaza del Triunfo; Catedral; Giralda; Patio de los Naranjos (see p.86); Parque de María Luisa (see p.85).

Tranquil reflections of palms and cypresses in the pools of the Poet's Garden.

Sevilla: La Cartuja

Location: Across the River Guadalquivir on the Isla de la Cartuja

open: Tue to Sun and Public Holidays (closes Mon except if a Public Holiday), 1 Apr to 30 Sep 11am–9pm and 1 Oct to 31 Mar 11am–7pm
open: As above

Further information from:
La Cartuja, Isla de la Cartuja, s/n, 41071 Sevilla
Tel: 95 448 06 11
Fax: 95 448 06 12

Nearby sights of interest:
Tile shops in the Triana district; Espacio Cultural Puerta Triana; Parque Temático; restored Expo 92 gardens.

The orange groves were restored in the early 1990s.

Dominated by the huge kiln chimneys that have been part of the history of this fascinating site on the banks of the River Guadalquivir, La Cartuja was splendidly restored and used as a major attraction during Seville's Expo 92.

From the 15th century the area was associated with the Carthusians who built the monastery complex and used the land for horticulture and agriculture. Christopher Columbus was a frequent visitor and the massive *Phytolacca dioica* is reputedly a plant he brought back from his voyages. In the 19th century an English industrialist built a ceramic factory on the site, returning it to its earlier usage. To a great extent he respected the character and layout and in the 1990s when it was prepared for the Expo, landscapers were able to restore or recreate elements of the earlier farm that had been on the site.

Today the citrus orchards, with standard trees, are laid out in the geometric patterning of the Moorish citrus groves seen in mosque patios. In courtyards near the entrance to La Cartuja there are block plantings of silvery-textured aromatic herbs, such as cotton lavender and lavender. Other fruit trees include olive, mulberry, damson, and apricot. For shade and ornament there are good plantings of tree of heaven (*Ailanthus altissima*), *Sophora japonica*, nettle tree (*Celtis australis*), and Judas tree (*Cercis siliquastrum*). Palms, including date palms and *Washingtonia filifera*, contribute to the Mediterranean atmosphere.

Sevilla: Parque de María Luisa

Location: SE of the city centre

Covering an area of 38ha (94 acres) the Parque de María Luisa is one of Seville's most delightful and interesting major parks. It was once part of the grounds of the Palacio de San Telmo, but was given to the people of the city in 1893 by María Luisa the Duchess of Montpensier.

It was laid out as a park and intended as the site for the ill-fated Ibero-American Exposition of 1914 (which eventually took place in 1929). The French landscape architect J C N Forestier was responsible for much of the park's design in the period before 1929. Many of the pavilions and sites for the Expo are still in use and one in particular, the Plaza de España, is one of the major attractions in the park. It has a semicircular canal between the large plaza and the brick pavilion behind it. All round the walls of the pavilion are tiled benches and murals, each representing one of Spain's provinces. The other major pavilion, the Plaza de América, built to include Mudéjar, Gothic, and Renaissance styles, houses the Museo de Artes y Costumbres Populares (Museum of Folk Arts and Traditions). Apart from these two main architectural features there are numerous other buildings and at least 20 *glorietas* named in honour of sculptors, artists, writers, and poets of all descriptions. Each *glorieta* comprises statuary, benches, and mature plantings of trees and shrubs.

Throughout the park there are massive specimens of *Magnolia grandiflora* and long shady avenues of planes. Water features are abundant with a landscaped lake at the centre of the park, complete with a domed island gazebo. Here there are real waterbirds but in one of the ponds ceramic ducks and frogs mingle with the feathered sort. To the edge of the park and bounded by the river is the Paseo de las Delicias, a smaller but equally attractive and well-designed public space.

open: At all times

Further information from:
Oficina de Turismo, Avenida de la Constitución, 21, Sevilla
Tel: 95 422 14 04

Nearby sights of interest:
Palacio de San Telmo (open by appointment); Universidad (former Royal Tobacco Factory); Hotel Alfonso XIII; Paseo de las Delicias; Reales Alcázares.

Part of the semicircular canal of the Plaza de España, built for the Ibero-American Exposition of 1929.

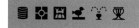

open: All year, Mon to Sat
10.30am–5pm and Sun
10.30am–1.30pm

Further information from:
Tourist Office, Avenida de
la Constitución 21, Sevilla
Tel: 95 422 14 04

Nearby sights of interest:
See below.

Serried ranks of orange trees.

 ## 19 *Sevilla: Patio de los Naranjos*

Location: Adjoining the cathedral of Seville

The Patio de los Naranjos and the minaret, now the cathedral's tower, La Giralda, are the only remaining features of Seville's 12th-century mosque. The patio or courtyard was associated with the traditional Muslim rituals of cleansing and meditation before prayer. At its centre is a fountain and basin, from which water overflows into the irrigation channels at the base of each of the hundreds of orange trees arranged in straight lines.

Today the courtyard, 3ha (7½ acres) in size, is a place to walk by, rather than to use, as it was in its heyday. Then the patio was used for Koranic teachings and provided shade, flower, fruit, and water. There were once gates to enter it on three sides but none is in use now and its purpose as a place to walk through for real and metaphoric cleansing, before entering the mosque, has been lost.

---

open: All year, daily,
9am–6pm
open: As above

Further information from:
Plaza de Pilatos 1, Sevilla
Tel: 95 422 52 98

Nearby sights of interest:
Catedral; Giralda; Jardines de
los Reales Alcázares (see p.83);
Hospital de los Venerables
Sacerdotes (see opposite);
Patio de los Naranjos (see above).

20 *Sevilla: Casa de Pilatos*

Location: E of the old quarter of Seville on Plaza de Pilatos

With a history reaching back to the 15th century the Casa de Pilatos provides a complete picture of the Mudéjar architecture on a relatively small and approachable scale, compared to that of the Alhambra for example. To see the several garden areas and patios it is necessary, fortunately, to visit the well-restored decorated rooms and salons on the lower floor of the house.

Softening the typically Andalusian covered walkway or *apeadero* are trails of climbers, including bougainvillea and plumbago. Orange blossom and fruits ornament the courtyard walls and arcades in season. Once they were trained into fan shapes, but many have grown away from the rigid control of the espalier system.

The main patio, although Moorish in effect, is a combination of many styles and includes Gothic and Renaissance elements. Its symmetry and geometric layout provide a peaceful meditative atmosphere emphasized by the marble fountain and basin at its centre. The tour takes you to the right of the patio and through several rooms and corridors before entering one of the most delightful enclosed palace gardens; known as the Jardín Chico, it

Portugal

Although the Portuguese island of Madeira has for a long time drawn visitors to its gardens and plants, the gardens on the mainland are among the country's distinctive yet little-known attractions. A mild winter climate with hot summers has given Portugal a green landscape, but the rugged, hilly, and in places, mountainous nature of the inland terrain has meant that gardens are smaller than those on Madeira and, in many cases, terraced.

Portugal is bounded to the north and east by Spain, but the vernacular of house and garden is not as you might expect. The Portuguese style has evolved from a similar base as the Spanish, with Roman, Moorish, and a Christian overlay of ideas, but the result is a unique use of elements from each culture that has influenced life in a country on the Atlantic edge of Europe.

One of the most fascinating sites is the excavated Roman city of Conimbríga (see p.113), where a peristyle garden has been reproduced. Although there are no whole landscapes or sites with Arabic designs several elements introduced by the Moors do remain in Portuguese gardens, but these have been adapted to suit the more domestic, intimate scale of their gardens. The most obvious of these is the use of ceramic tiles or *azulejos*, to give them their Arabic name. The Portuguese have used them in gardens to decorate benches, walls, arcades, and columns and, after the 15th century, instead of keeping to geometric designs on

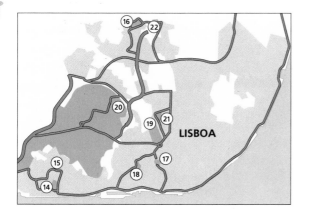

Plants appear to float on the surface of one of the water tanks at the Jardim Episcopal de Castelo Branco.

Box-lined paths in the Jardim do Museu dos Biscainhos, Braga, lead to shadehouses formed from clipped camellia bushes.

the tiles, they created pictures of plants, landscapes, and romantic adventures, as well as historic events.

The tiled *loggias* at the Palácio Fronteira (see pp.118–9) are among the most complete, but even these are suffering somewhat from the pollution of 20th-century life. The Quinta dos Azulejos (see p.116) has the most evocative tile garden. The Palácio Nacional de Queluz (see pp.132–5), too, has excellent examples of the delights of *azulejos*. To put the tiles in the garden into an historic framework visit the Museo Nacional do Azulejo, in the church and cloisters of Madre de Deus on Rua Madre de Deus 4.

The other Moorish feature that came into its own in the hands of Portuguese garden-makers is the water tank. Although it serves the purpose of conserving water for irrigation, in Portuguese gardens it has an explicitly ornamental intention. Usually it is backed by a highly decorated, arcaded *loggia* where you can sit and enjoy the shade and the water's reflections simultaneously. There is a distinctive example at Quinta da Bacalhoa (see p.107).

During the Renaissance a form of religious landscape developed at monasteries such as Tibães (see p.124), the sanctuary of Bom Jesus (see p.108), and in the forest

of Buçaco (see p.109), known as calvaries. Staircases, sometimes embellished with water cascades and usually very decorative, were built on steep hillsides. Each of the landings of the stairway was a Station of the Cross.

During the 16th century, when Portugal's independence from Spain was established, an obvious outcome was the proliferation of gardens with water tanks, *azulejos*, and French-style parterres in box. Terraces enclosed with box and, in some cases, with camellia became fashionable. Within the enclosures tapestries of topiary work were created. Camellias, imported from Japan at this time, thrived in Portugal. At Casa do Campo (see p.110) in the north there are famous camellia summerhouses and examples of centuries-old specimens of camellia.

In the 18th century wealth from Portugal's Brazilian colonies filtered through to society and in garden design, the long axis and wider spaces of the Baroque garden were introduced.

In 1755 an earthquake destroyed much of Lisbon and the resulting rebuilding of the city and life around it saw the creation of many *quintas* and their gardens, including the Quinta dos Azulejos (see p.116) and the Palácio dos Marquês de Pombal (see p.126). At this time botanic gardens such as those in Coimbra (see p.112) and in Lisbon (see p.116) were developed. The most splendid palace of this era is that of Queluz (see pp.132–5).

This century there is a programme to restore some of the country's historic gardens, among them the Jardim Botânico da Ajuda (see p.115). There is not yet a marked movement forward in terms of new design, but there is a modern garden of great importance that might well be the spring-board for new ideas. It is the Parque de Serralves (see pp.128–31), where the modernist style of house and garden are breathtaking in their harmony.

Irises and marginal water plants in the stream that meanders through the grounds of Lisbon's Parque do Museu Calouste Gulbenkian.

open: By appointment, at least 24 hours in advance

Further information from:
Señor Francisco Jácome de Vasconcelos, Quinto do Alão, Rua da Mainça 204, Leça do Balio, 4465 S Mamede de Infesta, Porto

Nearby sights of interest:
Parque de Serralves (see pp.128–31).

This fountain of a boy on a dolphin dates from the 18th century.

Quinta do Alão

Location: Off the Via Norte, 5km (3 miles) N of Oporto

The Quinta do Alão is referred to in documents dating from the 15th century and was once owned by the nearby Monastery of Leça do Balio. In the 17th century the property came into the ownership of the foster-sister of King Dom João IV. The house was remodelled and today still shows the characteristics of that era. Several large camellias, a *Magnolia grandiflora*, and other mature specimens dating from the garden's beginnings in the 1620s still survive. Also from that period, with later (18th-century) embellishments and additions by the Italian architect Nicolau Nasoni, are several stone pools with fountains, benches, and a canal system of irrigation. The camellias are among the earliest in Portuguese gardens, with circumferences of 2m (6½ft).

The garden is arranged in a series of three terraces. The formal parterre is filled with bulbs and annual bedding in season. Azaleas in salmon and apricot tones are planted in beds outside the parterre and in a new garden beyond the original garden wall, the present owner has established an attractive collection of shrubs, roses, and trees in a less formal planting style. The paths around the garden are shaded by camellias and other trees, but most lovely of all is the wisteria-clad pergola that runs along the length of the garden.

---

open: All year, Mon to Fri, 9am–5.30pm; on Sat, Sun, and Public Holidays the garden can be visited but cellars are closed and wine-tasting is not available

Further information from:
Quinta da Aveleda, Apartado 77, 4560 Penafiel
Tel: 055 711 10 41

Nearby sights of interest:
Casa de Mateus (see p.125); Vila Real.

Quinta da Aveleda

Location: 30km (18½ miles) NE of Oporto on A4 Oporto to Vila Real, exit at Penafiel Sul

Informality and romanticism are evident in abundance at Aveleda. The relaxed nature of the planting belies the careful choices of particular plants that offer an extended season of colour. In February the mimosa, *Acacia dealbata*, offers its fragrance and colour. In spring hybrid azaleas, rhododendrons, and camellias complete the floral picture in the woodland. Tiered plantings of these three shrubs make for a dramatically coloured avenue that leads towards the house.

The relaxed atmosphere of the woodland is heightened by gently winding paths, rustic cottages, and a lake complete with picturesque boat house, and a thatched duck house.

The garden opens up to a more formal grassed area lined with azaleas, making a strong contrast with the romanticism of the woodland. At the back of this immaculately kept lawn is a *chafariz* where water trickles constantly through a cracked pavement, giving succour to mosses and primulas.

The planting around the *quinta* is colourful with bulbs and flowering cherries in spring, followed by forget-me-nots, begonias, and pelargoniums. Clematis and wisteria, as well as roses, play an important ornamental role against house walls and on pergolas.

 # *Quinta da Bacalhoa*

Location: Vila Fresca de Azeitão, 12km (7½ miles) W of Setubal off the N10

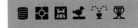

Quinta da Bacalhoa is a house with an historic past moving in and out of royal and noble ownership, which included Portugal's first Viceroy of the Indies, Afonso de Albuquerque, in 1528. It is to him the garden owes its Renaissance layout.

Entry to the property is through a wooden gate into a large courtyard, whose fine proportions prepare you a little for the drama and romance of the garden. As you step out through an archway into the garden, the symmetry and scale of the box parterre fills the immediate view. The soft green curves of box scrolls, fountains, and the climber-entwined walls of the house offer a peaceful haven, but a long raised walkway draws you onwards, past the round shapes of citrus trees in a sunken, old-style orange grove and numerous tiled wall benches, to the limpid waters of the water tank. Dominated on one side by an attractively roofed and arcaded pavilion, the parapets around the tank command views over the whole estate including the vineyard.

open: All year, daily, 11am–1pm; groups or coach parties should apply in advance to the address below

Further information from:
Martin J H Reynolds, 16 Largo da Academia Nacional de Belas Artes, 1200 Lisboa
Tel: 01 346 22 77

Nearby sights of interest:
Quinta das Torres (see p.139).

The soft, green curves of the intricate parterre contrast with the orange grove and water tank beyond.

Jardim do Museu dos Biscainhos

Location: Rua dos Biscainhos, Braga

open: All year, Tue to Sun, 10am–12.15pm and 2–5.30pm; closes Public Holidays
open: Museum: as above

Further information from:
Museu dos Biscainhos, Rua dos Biscainhos, 4700 Braga
Tel: 053 32 76 45

Nearby sights of interest:
Casa dos Biscainhos Museu; Sé (Braga Cathedral); Bom Jesus do Monte (see below); Mosteiro de São Martinho de Tibães (see p.124); Jardim de Santa Bárbara, Braga.

The buildings of the Palácio dos Biscainhos have been recorded since the mid-17th century, with the original garden of three distinct areas, formal, orchard, and vegetable, arriving in the 18th century. The Palácio is now a museum devoted to the furnishings and style of the period. The walled formal garden is still well maintained, but the other areas lack their former purposefulness. Box hedges enclose bright annuals, flowers tumble from urns, and water plays gently in the many fountains and pools of this formal area. One of the most delightful features, found in several gardens in the region, are the Casas de Fresco (cool places), which are made from camellias grown against strong wooden frames and shaped to form plant-roofed houses, with windows and doorways cut in the side "walls".

Bom Jesus do Monte

Location: 5km (3 miles) E of Braga on the N103

open: All year, daily, 8am–8pm
open: As above; closes Sat

Further information from:
Confrario do Bom Jesus do Monte, 4700 Braga
Tel: 053 67 66 36

Nearby sights of interest:
Citania de Briteiros.

Either side of the Baroque stairway there are attractive plantings.

The sanctuary gardens and Baroque staircase of Bom Jesus do Monte were begun in 1723 by the Archbishop of Braga. The individual tiers and galleries of the granite staircases, and white plastered walls seem to dissolve and become one architectural image leading the eye up the hill to the church at the top.

The sanctuary landscapes of the *escaderia* or Baroque staircases in Portugal have their origins in the Stations of the Cross. Some visitors use them in that way, for pilgrimages, while others take advantage of the half-hourly funicular and view the symbolic fountains and neatly kept terraces in passing. Here, surrounded by woodland, many visitors spend time picnicking or walking.

Topiary work is in box and camellia, and rhododendrons make a bright show in spring. Bom Jesus is crowded at weekends and during holidays, but on quieter days it is possible to feel the grandeur and scale of the enterprise.

Mata Nacional do Buçaco

Location: On the N235, 25km (15½ miles) from Coimbra

Entered through one of the many gateways in the stone wall that encompasses its 105ha (259 acres), Buçaco Forest offers the visitor an undulating, ancient landscape. The original oak and pine forest was the site of a Benedictine hermitage in the 6th century. Its present landscape and plantings date from the middle of the 17th century, when Barefoot Carmelites built their convent and the stone wall that surrounds the forest. Their love of nature resulted in a Papal Bull threatening anyone who damaged a tree with excommunication, thus ensuring the forest's continued survival.

Buçaco is now a blend of imported exotic trees, such as cedar, *Cupressus lusitanicus* (known here as Buçaco cedar), ginkgos, Japanese camphor trees, palms, sequoias, and native plants. In the understorey camellia, clivias, hydrangeas, lilies, mimosa, phillyrea, rhododendron, tree ferns, and heathers luxuriate.

There are many viewpoints, or *miradouros*, and monuments as well as hermitages to discover on one of several routes of varying length and timing. Try to see Vale dos Fetos (the Valley of Tree Ferns) and the nearby lake, Lago do Vale dos Fetos. The Fonte Fria (Cold Fountain) is also an evocative sight, with water flowing down 144 steps to a pool. Most dramatic of all buildings within the forest is the Palace Hotel. Once a hunting lodge, it was built between 1888 and 1908 near the site of the Carmelite Convent. A wisteria-clad pergola and a neatly clipped parterre are part of the hotel's contribution to the horticulture of the forest.

open: All year, daily
open: Sat to Thu; guided tours at specific times

Further information from:
Tourist Board of Luso-Buçaco, R Emídio Navarro, Luso, 3050 Mealhada
Tel: 031 93 91 33

Nearby sights of interest:
Hotel Palácio do Buçaco; Convento dos Carmelitas Descalços; Monument to the Battle of Buçaco; spa town of Luso.

The parterre in the grounds of the Buçaco Palace Hotel.

open: By appointment

Further information from:
Señora Maria Armanda Meirelles,
Casa do Campo, Molares,
4890 Celorico de Basto
Tel and fax: 055 36 12 31

Nearby sights of interest:
Bom Jesus do Monte (see p.108);
Mosteiro de São Martinho de
Tibães (see p.124); Jardim do
Museu dos Biscainhos (see p.108);
Parque Natural de Alvão.

Columns of clipped camellias
guard the entrance to the
garden terrace.

Casa do Campo

Location: NE of Oporto near Celorico de Basto in the Tamego River Valley

Topiary work in camellias of great age and size is the striking characteristic of the gardens at Casa do Campo. In the gardens of northern Portugal topiary is not uncommon, but it is the use of camellias as the base material that sets it apart from the usual. At Casa do Campo the garden is on a terrace above a courtyard and at one time could only be reached via a Venetian-style bridge from the house. The topiary shapes tower to 9m (30ft) above the courtyard, and cast long and shapely shadows across its sandy surface.

The garden is divided into eight rather open parterres with double box hedges. There are several Casas de Fresco (cool places) of camellias shaped into shadehouses. They have been grown on sturdy wooden frames to support the windows, doorways, and pitched roofs. The central camellia "room" differs from the others in that it has no "roof". Instead it is a circular structure with arched doorways and windows. Its curvaceous shape emphasizes the stone pool at its centre.

Although clipped the camellias still flower, producing fragrant and colourful blooms from January through to March, and they are followed by rhododendrons, also shaped, offering spring colour.

There are bed-and-breakfast facilities at the modest manor house which has elements of Baroque and Renaissance style. There is a chapel attached to the manor house.

8 *Jardim Episcopal de Castelo Branco*

Location: Near the Spanish border; 262km (163 miles) from Lisbon

The gardens of the Bishop's Palace date back to 1725. Plants and stone statuary vie for attention in this formal garden designed by Dom João de Mendonca. The statuary represents zodiacal symbols, the Four Seasons and Four Virtues, and Kings and Queens of Portugal, as well as the Apostles.

The formal terrace is dominated by statuary and neatly clipped box hedges of great age, and from here two stairways lead up to a higher level with large water tanks and fountains. Most dramatic of all is the scrolled, arabesque flower island in one of the tanks, evocative of the beds set in water at the Roman site at Conimbríga (see p.113).

open: All year, daily, 9am to sunset; closes 25 Dec, 1 Jan, and Good Friday

Further information from:
Câmara Municipal de Castelo Branco, 6000 Castelo Branco
Tel: 072 33 03 30

Nearby sights of interest:
Museu Francisco Tavares Proença Júnior; Miradouro de São Gens.

9 *Jardim do Cerco*

Location: 40km (25 miles) NW of Lisbon on the N9

Jardim do Cerco lies behind and adjacent to the Palace of Mafra. Work commenced on the Palace, which was originally built as a monastery and basilica, in 1717, and it is likely that when the building was completed in 1735 the formal gardens, the avenues, and other features of the garden were in place.

The garden is a buffer between the forest hunting grounds of Mafra and the Palace. Formal box-edged beds hold roses and there are large topiary accents. There are the remains of an aqueduct and a waterwheel, together with several large pools.

open: Daily, 9am to sunset

Further information from:
Câmara Municipal de Mafra, Tourist Information, Av 25 de Abril, Mafra
Tel: 061 81 20 23

Nearby sights of interest:
Palácio Nacional de Mafra; village of Sobreiro for ceramics.

Urns holding summer bedding punctuate the different levels of the terraced gardens.

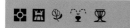

open: Daily, summer
9am–9pm and winter
9am–5.30pm

Further information from:
Jardim Botânico da Universidade
de Coimbra, Arcos do Jardim,
3049 Coimbra, Codex
Tel: 039 82 28 97

Nearby sights of interest:
Mosteiro de Santa Cruz and
Jardim da Manga (a cloister
garden); Parque de Santa Cruz;
Portugal dos Pequenitos; university
campus; old town and Sé Velha
(old cathedral); Quinta das
Lagrimas; Roman Peristyle
Garden (see opposite).

From the central box-lined
paths there are views up to
the glasshouses.

10 *Jardim Botânico de Coimbra*

Location: Alameda Dr Júlio Henriques near aquaduct, to the E of university campus

The botanical garden was created during the 18th century as part of the Marquês de Pombal's modernizing reform of Coimbra University. William Elsden was commissioned to design the 20ha (49 acre) site; work began in 1772 and by 1774 the garden was established. Originally on a steep slope, the garden was levelled and terraced and is much the same today as when first laid out except that now the trees are mature. Because of the value of the plant collection the garden was walled and is entered through three large ornamental gates, dating from 1791 to 1794.

The garden is on several levels, the uppermost comprising taxonomic beds for botanic study. You can walk around three sides of the garden on a wide balustraded upper terrace with single seats set into the wall. Several double stairways descend into the main, roughly rectangular, central area, where there are numerous small, circular, and asymmetrical beds all edged with 60cm (24in) high box hedges. Box domes and pyramids in the hedging mark the start of paths or meeting points of several paths. The beds hold ornamental plants, including roses and clivias. Height, shape, colour, and texture, as well as shade, are offered by the numerous mature flowering trees growing in various beds. Looking up from the central part of the garden you can see the delicate-looking iron and glass structure of the glasshouses, which dominate this area. At the centre of the lower terrace is a circular pool, with a fountain, fish, and waterlilies.

The best way to gain an overall impression of the garden is to walk along the three sides of the upper terrace, enjoying the shade of avenues of limes, *Tilia europaea*. There are at least 40 species of eucalyptus and a large Moreton Bay fig, *Ficus macrophylla*; a collection of *Araucaria* and many plants from California, South Africa, and South America. The breadth of the collection is the result of the exchanges of plant and seed undertaken by the garden's 19th-century Director, Júlio Henriques (Director 1873–1918) with Baron von Mueller of Melbourne Botanical Garden.

The garden was opened to the public in the 19th century and as well as botanical plantings, purely ornamental groupings were made to show how such plants looked in action.

Conimbríga: Roman Peristyle Garden

Location: In the grounds of Museu Monográfico de Conimbríga, 3km (2 miles) SE of Condeixa and 16km (10 miles) SW of Coimbra

open: Daily, Apr to Aug 9am–1pm and 2–8pm and Sep to Mar 9am–1pm and 2–6pm
open: Apr to Aug, Tue to Sun, 10am–1pm and 2–7pm; Sep to Mar as above but closes 6pm

Further information from:
Museu Monográfico de Conimbríga, Conimbríga, 3750 Condeixa-a-Nova
Tel: 039 94 11 77

Nearby sights of interest:
Excavations at Rabaçal and Coimbra.

Conimbríga is the most important Roman site in Portugal, although it was probably a Celto-Iberian site before its Roman history. It owes its survival (as an excavated site) to the fact that it was abandoned in the mid-6th century.

Although, in the modern sense, there is no garden to visit here, the site is well worth seeing in itself. As an excavated landscape with wildflowers thrusting through piles of Roman roadstone, it has a dramatic beauty and there is a recreation of a peristyle garden in one of the houses.

The rectangular tank or pool was at the colonnaded heart of the Roman home. Set into the water are curving beds, here planted with irises and herbs. Some 40 jets of water play across the waterways between the scrolled-bed edges, offering an insight into the atmosphere such a garden or courtyard held.

The house is resplendent with many mosaics and the islands of floral colour appearing to float on the water seem to mimic the tapestry effects on the floors. Unfortunately this area has had to be protected from the elements and is roofed over with an unappealing DIY shed-like roof.

That apart, these fragments of an ancient past seem so bright set in relief against blue skies and olive-clad hills.

The restored gardens in the House of the Fountains.

Jardim do Palácio de Estói

Location: In the town square of Estói, 9km (5½ miles) N of Faro

open: All year, Tue to Sat, 9am–12.30pm and 2–5.30pm; closes Public Holidays

Further information from:
Câmara Municipal de Faro
Tel: 089 82 20 42

Nearby sights of interest:
Roman ruins at Milreu; Faro: Museu Municipal; Museu Marítimo; Castelo de Silves.

The peach-coloured Palácio de Estói is closed to the public but its garden, with shady avenues of palms and terraced levels linked by balustraded and elaborately tiled staircases, is open. Gazebos and classical columns, statuary, and rectangular lakes or water tanks add to a romantic atmosphere. It is possible that the palace will be restored and eventually opened to the public.

Casa da Insua

Location: A few km before Penalva do Castelo on the N3291 N from Mangualde

open: All year, daily,
9am–6pm; closes 25 Dec, 1 Jan,
and Easter

Further information from:
Señor José Joaquim Olazabal
Albuquerque, 3550 Penalva
do Castelo, Beira Alta

Nearby sights of interest:
Medieval town of Mangualde;
city of Viseu; Parque Natural de
Serra da Estrela.

This privately owned country house, also known as Solar dos Albuquerques, and garden is in the Dâo wine region mid-way between Oporto and the Spanish border. The parterre garden in front of the house's main façade is set on two terraces. Its arrangement is very complicated with a number of geometric compartments. At the centre is a shadehouse made by the skilful shaping of camellia hedges. The parterre shapes are made in clipped box with pyramids marking the corners of each section. These are filled with strong plantings of roses and cannas.

This geometric manipulation is in stark contrast to the larger, outer garden area, known as the Woodland or English Garden, where glades, rides, walks, bridges, and animal houses are among the focal features. Both the house and garden probably date from the late 18th century and some of the architectural work is attributable to students, or followers, of the celebrated Italian architect, Nicolau Nasoni.

Lisboa: Jardim–Museu Agrícola Tropical

Location: In Belém district near the waterfront to the W of the city centre

open: All year, daily except Mon
and Public Holidays, 10am–5pm

Further information from:
Ministry of Science and
Technology; Jardim-Museu
Agrícola Tropical, Calçada do
Galvão, Belém, 1400 Lisboa

Nearby sights of interest:
Mosteiro dos Jeronimos; Jardim
Botânico da Ajuda (see opposite).

Flowers of the Brazilian coral tree.

Once known as the Jardim do Ultramar or the Colonial Gardens, this garden holds the basic collection of plants brought to Portugal from its mostly tropical or subtropical colonies of the past. There is also a tropical Agricultural Museum from the former Palácio dos Condes da Calheta, which houses vegetative material from the colonies. The museum and garden have been on this site since 1914. Given the garden's *raison d'être* as a place for testing the hardiness of new introductions, there are some interesting adaptations to the garden's 18th-century original layout.

Stately avenues of broad-leaved trees were replanted with the majestic Australian king palm (*Archontophoenix alexandrae*); today many are over 21m (39ft). Canary Island date palms (*Phoenix canariensis*) take the lead in another avenue, while Brazilian queen palms and *Chorisia speciosa* make a stunning combination along yet another. Bright-red flowerheads of Brazilian coral trees (*Erythrina crista-galli*) create a glowing flame-like display down the long avenue back to the entrance. There are also good collections of Australian trees, including casuarina, eucalyptus, and ficus.

 Lisboa: Jardim Botânico da Ajuda

Location: In Belém, on the western side of the city

Restoration work began on the Jardim Botânico da Ajuda in 1993 and in 1997 it was reopened to the public. It was founded in 1772 as the Royal Botanic Garden. The Italian, Domingo Vandelli, who was in charge of its construction and layout, was appointed Director in 1791. During his directorship he imported seeds and plants from all over the world, totalling some 5,000 species. It was first opened to the public in the early 19th century when its hothouses were constructed.

Laid out in terraces overlooking the River Tagus, it is a formal garden with box-hedged parterres, fountains, pools, and statuary. In the central fountain water spouts from the heads of cobras, fish, frogs, and ducks, with sealions and seahorses in attendance.

Old and statuesque specimen trees on the upper terrace, including a sizeable dragon-tree (*Dracaena draco*), silky oak (*Grevillea robusta*), and *Schotia latifolia*, have all been retained. Former botanical family beds have been modernized and a chequer-board-style layout highlights plant collections with particular relevance in Portugal's history.

A new addition is a herb garden with access and labelling for blind and disabled visitors.

open: Mon to Fri, 8am–5pm; closes Public Holidays

Further information from:
Jardim Botânico da Ajuda,
Calcada da Ajuda, 1300 Lisboa
Tel: 01 363 81 61
Fax: 01 362 25 03

Nearby sights of interest:
Jardim-Museu Agrícola Tropical; Torre de Belém; Palácio Nacional da Ajuda; Museu Nacional dos Coches; Planetário Calouste Gulbenkian.

In the central fountain water gushes from the heads of cobras, fish, and other creatures.

open: All year except Aug, Mon to Fri, 8am–6pm

Further information from:
Secretário-General Colégio Manuel Bernardes, Quinta dos Azulejos, Paço do Lumiar, Rua Esquerda, 1600 Lisboa
Tel: 01 757 05 01
Fax: 01 757 23 11

Nearby sights of interest:
Parque do Monteiro-Mor (see p.120); Museu Nacional do Traje.

16 *Lisboa: Quinta dos Azulejos*

Location: In the village of Lumiar, now in the greater conurbation N of Lisbon

An historic *quinta* dating from the 18th century, Quinta dos Azulejos became a private school in 1935 and at that time it was considered far enough away from Lisbon to be a country boarding school. Today, as Lisbon has spread, it is very much an urban school. Although the serpentine architecture and extensive tilework of the tile garden built here between 1779 and 1780 are now part of the school's playground, they are much-loved by the staff and children. A central walkway with pillars is shaded by a rampant yellow bignonia. Roses climb the pergola and there are box-edged beds. There is some deterioration, but it is delightful to see 20th-century children so at home in the playground of 18th-century sophisticates.

open: Summer, Mon to Fri 9am–8pm and Sat, Sun, and Public Holidays 10am–8pm; winter, Mon to Fri closes 6pm and Sat, Sun, and Public Holidays closes 4pm

Further information from:
Faculdade da Ciência, Universidade de Lisboa, Rua da Escola Politécnica, Lisboa

Nearby sights of interest:
Parque de Eduardo VII.

A pool on the garden's upper level.

17 *Lisboa: Jardim Botânico, Universidade de Lisboa*

Location: In the city centre a few minutes from the Avenida da Liberdade

Founded in 1874 when it superseded the Jardim Botânico da Ajuda (see p.115) in importance, the garden covers 4ha (10 acres) and is still connected to the Faculty of Science of Lisbon University. It has an entrance in the campus and another at its lower end, reached after a gentle descent into glades and avenues of palms.

Over 2,500 species are cultivated here. Plant families in box-edged beds are located at the top part of the garden, where there is also an observatory and a raised stone-edged pool. Among the eye-catching plants are vast plantings of *Geranium maderense*. Steps lead down onto the sloping landscape of the garden, and groves of giant cacti and an avenue of palms curve around one side of it. At the garden's centre is a collection of woodland trees, including exotics such as dombeya, *Metrosideros excelsa*, bamboos in great thickets, and a vast *Chorisia speciosa*. Although the garden is in the midst of a bustling traffic-crowded city, the woodland is home to birds and the effect of their song evokes a sense of the countryside.

Lisboa: English Cemetery

Location: In the Estrêla quarter in the city centre

Although not a garden in the strictest sense, the English Cemetery is a tranquil, densely planted, historic site. Cypresses and Judas trees (*Cercis siliquastrum*) provide much of the shade cover in what Virginia Woolf described in 1905 as "a most lovely place, sweet with flowers and so hot and shady and green that we stayed there a long time".

The English Cemetery was first used in 1725. It is a place for fascinating reflection about the lives of expatriots of the past and more recent times. One of its most celebrated tombs is that of the author Henry Fielding.

Pelargonium, bougainvillea, and irises flower in pots and on graves. Palms and pines, as well as flowering trees, offer a balance between sombre shadows and dappled dancing sunlight.

Of particular note are the box-edged and box-filled grave gardens, putting box into its historic context as a coffin wood.

open: Ring bell for gatekeeper; no charge, although a donation to the gatekeeper might be welcome

Further information from:
International War Graves Commission or The Vicarage, Rua de São Jorge, Lisboa

Nearby sights of interest:
Estrêla Basilica; Complexo das Amoreiras (post-modern shopping centre); Casa das Águas and Aqueducto das Águas Livres; Jardim Botânico, Universidade de Lisboa (see opposite).

Box lines and fills many of the graves in this tranquil setting.

19 *Lisboa: Estufa Fria and Estufa Quente*

Location: In the NW corner of Parque de Eduardo VII in Lisbon central area

open: All year, daily; Estufa Fria 9am–5pm, Estufa Quente 9am–4.30pm, Lake 9am–4.30pm; closes 1 Jan, 25 Apr, 1 May, 25 Dec

Nearby sights of interest:
Parque do Museu Calouste Gulbenkian (see opposite); Praça do Marquês de Pombal.

Arums thrive near one of the indoor pools.

Although usually described simply as the Estufa Fria, there are three distinct areas to enjoy. The inner part, roofed with glass, supported on palm-trunk-like pillars is the Estufa Quente (opened in 1975), which offers protective cover to a range of greenhouse and conservatory plants, such as amaryllis, bromeliads, clivias, and strelitzia. The Estufa Fria is a cool greenhouse, which, with its simple lath roof offers shade rather than the warmer, humid conditions of the Estufa Quente. Rhododendron, camellia, and bougainvillea thrive in the cool, dappled shade. Opened in 1930 the Estufa Fria is the largest wooden lath house in the world, and is about 280m (919ft) in height and 1ha (2½ acres) in area.

Both Estufas are built into a former quarry in the north-west part of Parque de Eduardo VII. Outside the Estufas is the third area of the garden, a lake with islands, statuary, and duckhouses. Walls of the quarry buildings are covered in bougainvillea and fragrant clouds of the yellow Banksian rose.

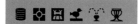

20 *Lisboa: Jardim do Palácio Fronteira*

Location: In Benfica, a northern suburb of Lisbon, just on the northern edge of the Parque Florestal de Monsanto

open: Daily except Sun and Public Holidays at specified times; Jun to Sep, tours of the Palace and grounds take place on the half hour from 10.30am until 12 noon; Oct to May, two tours each morning at 11am and 12 noon
open: As above

Further information from:
Fundação das Casas de Fronteira e Alorna, Largo São Domingos de Benfica 1, 1500 Lisboa

Nearby sights of interest:
Jardim Zoológico; Benfica Stadium; Parque Florestal de Monsanto.

Formality on a grand scale with all the characteristics of Portuguese garden architecture is the hallmark of the Jardim do Palácio Fronteira. It was established in the late 17th century and written of in flowing terms in 1669 by two Florentine tourists of note, Cosimo de Medici and the Marchese Corsini. Their description of it as a garden with "diverse parterres, statues, and bas reliefs" holds good for the garden of the 21st century. But its maturity and the weathering of the architectural elements evoke their own brand of romanticism.

Although it is possible to visit the garden exclusively, it is more satisfying to progress through the highly decorated public and some private rooms of the Palace, all the while catching glimpses of bold foliage, tilework, and flowers through windows. Once outdoors there is a terrace or promenade, the Chapel Promenade, with statuary, arches, niches, and tiled panels, that leads to a chapel. The terrace overlooks the Jardim de Venus where mature trees, camellias, and ferns luxuriate. A bunya-bunya pine (*Araucaria bidwillii*) makes a strong outline, towering above the garden. A shell- and china-encrusted grotto-like house, Casa de Fresco or do Água, is also to be found in this part of the garden. Some of the porcelain is in the form of whole plates, once used at royal banquets in the late 17th century. In front of the Casa de Fresco is a tank or pool with curved scrolled benches or walkways.

But the major attraction is the Jardim Grande, a geometric parterre of squares, diamonds, stars, and wedges, which covers 3,700 sq m (39,712 sq ft). At its back is a large limpid water tank with an architecturally balanced viewing gallery, Galeria dos Reis. As they did when the garden was first laid out, the tilework, the architecture of the Galeria and tank (complete with grottoes and ballustrading), and the immaculately kept box-hedged parterres continue to make an unforgettable impact on the garden's visitors.

The Galeria dos Reis overlooks the large water tank.

21 *Lisboa: Parque do Museu Calouste Gulbenkian*

Location: N of the Parque de Eduardo VII

open: All year, daily, 9am–7pm; closes Public Holidays

Further information from:
Fundação Calouste Gulbenkian, Avenida Berna, 45, 1067 Lisboa
Tel: 01 793 51 31

Nearby sights of interest:
Parque de Eduardo VII; Estufa Fria and Estufa Quente (see opposite); Praça do Marquês de Pombal; Museu Calouste Gulbenkian; Centro de Arte Moderna (Gulbenkian Museum of Modern Art).

The Museu Calouste Gulbenkian was inauguarated in 1969 and is set in the parkland of the former Palácio Azambuja or dos Meninos de Palhavã, which since 1918 has been the site of the Spanish Embassy.

The modern park completed in 1969 is overlaid on a 19th-century plan by Jacob Weiss. The buildings and layout, although 20th century, adhere to naturalistic landscape principles and are the work of landscape architects Robeiro Telles and Viana Barreto. Their design achieved a careful balance of buildings within the landscape. Sweeping lawns follow the natural contours of the land down to the central lake, where you can meander on paths and bridges across stream inlets planted with irises and waterside marginals.

Statuary and sculptures make good focal points, as does the amphitheatre. The planting scheme is also naturalistic with stands of feathery pampas grass, the small-leaved Brazilian pepper tree (*Schinis terebinthus*), ribbon gum, and Turkey oak. Eucalyptus and poplars offer shade and shimmering movement, while shrub plantings provide cover and privacy. There is also a rose garden.

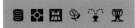

Further information from:
Museu Nacional do Traje, Parque do Monteiro-Mor, Largo Júlio de Castilho, 1600 Lisboa
Tel: 01 759 03 18
Fax: 01 759 12 24

Nearby sights of interest:
Museu Nacional do Traje (Portuguese domestic fashions and costume); Museu Nacional do Teatro.

22 *Lisboa: Parque do Monteiro-Mor*

Location: 2km (1¼ mile) N of Lisbon in the suburb of Lumiar

Parque do Monteiro-Mor has a formidable horticultural and botanical pedigree. In the 18th century it was the residence of the Keeper of the Royal Forests. The planting began under the third Marques of Angeja, and by 1763 Monteiro-Mor was well known for its plant collections. In 1840 the Marques of Palmela acquired the properties, and subsequent generations of his family relied on the services of several distinguished botanists including Rosenfelder, Friedrich Welwitsch, and Jacob Weiss. The microclimate here, on a north-facing slope with abundant springs, allows for the growth of trees and shrubs from different climates, including a Moreton Bay fig (*Ficus macrophylla*) and a white mulberry (*Morus alba*). Among the splendid mature trees are towering specimens of *Platanus* x *acerifolia*, the New Zealand Christmas tree (*Meterosideros excelsa*), and a Norfolk Island pine (*Araucaria excelsa*).

Further information from:
Quinta da Boa Vista, Lomba da Boa Vista, Funchal

Nearby sights of interest:
Quinta do Palheiro Ferreiro (see p.123); Jardim Tropical da Quinta do Monte Palace (see p.122).

Part of the orchid collection.

23 *Madeira: Quinta da Boa Vista*

Location: On the outskirts of Funchal on the EN101

The gardens were established when the house was built over 200 years ago. It has been in the Garton family for over a century and is famed for its orchid collection. The growing of orchids here leads back to England in the 1920s when Sir William Cooke began to establish orchids at his Berkshire estate, Wyld Court. His fine private collection grew into Wyld Court Orchids, known around the world to orchid enthusiasts. In the 1970s his daughter Betty visited Madeira and met Cecil Garton, recipient of some Wyld Court orchids. They married and the Boa Vista collection developed from their mutual interest in the plants.

The *quinta* gardens contain a collection of Australian bottle brushes (*Callistemon* spp.), South African aloes, and bromeliads from South America. There are also many Madeiran natives, including *Geranium maderense*. The focal point of a visit is, of course, the Orchid Houses. *Cymbidium*, *Lycastes*, and Slipper orchids (*Paphiopedilum*) are the predominant genera. All through the year there are exhibits of other showy hybrids and rare species.

Madeira: Jardim Botânico da Madeira

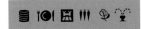

Location: 3km (2 miles) from Funchal centre on Caminho do Meio

Jardim Botânico da Madeira began as the private garden of the Quinta do Bom Sucesso owned by the Reid family and was laid out in 1881. Several of the mature specimen trees from that era have been preserved. The garden was moved to its present site in 1960 and today the *quinta* is used as a research laboratory. The gardens, 3.5ha (8½ acres) in size, are on a steeply sloping site with panoramic views over the Bay of Funchal and the surrounding mountains. Over 2,000 plants, including bromeliads, cacti, conifers, ferns, orchids, palms, and flowering trees and shrubs, such as azaleas and magnolias, are grown here. Near the house is a collection of 100 indigenous species, including those found on exposed slopes and in Madeira's laurel woodlands. Among them are *Apollonias barbujana*, *Laurus azorica*, and *Persea indica*. Included in the exotic species in the garden are acacia, arums, anthurium, begonia, callistemon, cycads, and roses.

Part of the botanic garden's remit is to collect a representative range of plants for educational, scientific, and economic purposes. To this end there is a well-established collection of citrus and subtropical fruit trees, such as avocado, custard apple, guava, and mango. Here too are Madeiran food plants, including sugar cane, sweet potato, and yam.

One of the most striking formal features is a plant tapestry, several hundred square metres in size, made up of a chessboard of coloured foliage. It is best viewed from a higher vantage point.

open: All year, daily, 8am–6pm; closes 25 Dec

Further information from:
Jardim Botânico da Madeira, Caminho do Meio, Quinta do Bom Sucesso, 9050 Funchal, Madeira

Nearby sights of interest:
Quinta do Palheiro Ferreiro (see p.123); Jardim Tropical da Quinta do Monte Palace (see p.122); Quinta da Boa Vista (see opposite).

The tapestry of coloured foliage plants is best viewed from the upper terrace.

25 *Madeira: Quinta das Cruzes*

Location: On the outskirts of Funchal on Calçada do Pico

open: All year, Mon to Sat, 10am–12.30pm and 2–6pm; closes Public Holidays

Further information from:
Quinta das Cruzes, Museu das Cruzes, Calçada do Pico 1, Funchal
Tel: 091 74 13 82

Nearby sights of interest:
Quinta do Palheiro Ferreiro (see p.123); Jardim Tropical da Quinta do Monte Palace (see below); Quinta da Boa Vista (see p.120); Jardim Botânico da Madeira (see p.121); Museu das Cruzes.

The *quinta* dates from the 17th to the 18th century, but was restored and established as a museum of decorative arts in the 19th century. The garden holds many mature specimens of native and exotic plants, including *Agathis australis*, cycads, the dragon-tree (*Dracaena draco*), eucalyptus, jacaranda, kauri pine, laurels, mimosa, and the cheese plant (*Monstera deliciosa*). There is a fern collection and a good selection of orchids.

Many architectural features including tombstones and windows from archaeological sites are on display in the garden, and there are several pools, fountains, and water channels.

26 *Madeira: Jardim Tropical da Quinta do Monte Palace*

Location: In Monte, a mountain resort 6km (3¾ miles) from Funchal

open: All year, Mon to Sat, 9am–6pm

Further information from:
Fundação José Berardo, Monte Palace PO Box 280, Caminho do Monte, 174, 9050 Funchal
Tel: 091 78 23 39

Nearby sights of interest:
Quinta do Palheiro Ferreiro (see opposite); Jardim Botânico da Madeira (see p.121); Quinta das Cruzes (see above).

The lake is home to swans.

The Monte Palace was a luxury hotel but has been closed as such since the mid-1940s. The land was purchased by a local businessman, José Berardo, who restored the garden, opening it to the public in 1989. The former hotel building is now the headquarters of the Berardo Foundation, which provides grants for various projects and has funded the illustrations for the publication *Flora of Madeira* (Press, Short, & Turland, 1994).

The garden covers 7ha (17 acres) and consists of undulating landscape filled with many mature trees and shrubs, viewpoints, picnic areas, a lake, various ponds, and several collections of plants. The most important of these is the cycads, numbering over 700 species and varieties, mostly made up of *Encephalartos* sp. from South Africa. Some of the plants are among the most ancient still living and are said to be up to 1,000 years old. Other collections include azaleas, heathers, orchids, proteas, and tree ferns. There is also a section devoted to Madeiran flora. Throughout the garden there are various "themed" areas where porcelain, and oriental and Portuguese tiles are on permanent display.

27 *Madeira: Quinta do Palheiro Ferreiro*

Location: 9km (5½ miles) from Funchal on the EN102 to Camacha

open: All year, Mon to Fri, 9.30am–12.30pm; closes 25 Dec, 1 Jan, Easter, 1 May

Further information from:
Quinta do Palheiro, São Gonçalo, 9050 Funchal
Tel: 091 79 22 14

Nearby sights of interest:
Jardim Tropical da Quinta do Monte Palace (see opposite); Jardim Botânico da Madeira (see p.121); Quinta das Cruzes (see p.122).

Also known as Blandy's Garden after the English family that has owned it since 1884, the garden was originally laid out earlier in the 19th century for the property's first owner the Conde de Carvalhal. Oak and plane tree avenues, as well as newly imported trees from South America and New Zealand, were among the early plantings. The Count fled to England in 1828, returning in 1834 fired with enthusiasm for the ideals of the English landscape park. The overall layout of the garden reflects this, and many of the now mature trees and the camellia collection date from this era. In 1884/5 the property was sold to the Blandy family, the owners of Blandy Brothers which is a large company with interests in wine, shipping, and tourism. In the early days fruit trees and orchards were replaced by garden areas, of which there are four principal sections.

The main garden in front of the New House (built in 1891) has a rock bank planted with interesting Australian and South African species, including proteas. A flight of steps leads down to a sunken garden with an octagonal pool and clipped-box topiary. A long border lines the route to a small topiary garden, Jardim da Senhora (the Ladies' Garden), thought to be the oldest garden on the site. Near the chapel are long rectangular ponds and sweeping lawns. On the other side of the sunken garden is an area known as the Inferno. It is a small, steep valley holding indigenous Madeiran species, as well as tree ferns, camellias, and rhododendrons.

The Sunken Garden was laid out in the 1940s by Mildred Blandy, mother of the present owner and a formidable plantswoman, who introduced many species from the southern hemisphere to the garden. The estate as a whole covers 325ha (803 acres) and the garden some 12ha (30 acres).

One of the most dramatic features is the kilometre-long entrance drive to the garden. Lined with old varieties of camellia, it is a delight during the flowering period from December to April.

Formality and humour in the closely clipped figures in Jardim da Senhora.

open: By appointment

Further information from:
Quinta da Palmeira, Rua
de Levada de Santa Luzia,
9000 Funchal

Nearby sights of interest:
Jardim Tropical da Quinta do
Monte Palace (see p.122); Jardim
Botânico da Madeira (see p.121).

Tiles are among the wall features.

28 *Madeira: Quinta da Palmeira*

Location: On the Rua de Levada de Santa Luzia, overlooking Funchal

The garden at Quinta de Palmeira has been owned by several generations of the English family Welch. It is on a precipitous site and overlooks Funchal. A long, steep walk leads up from the road past a small grotto. On either side of the path plants hug the walls and grow from cracks and crannies in it, among them aloes and succulents. As you would expect on such a steep slope, the garden is terraced and pelargoniums spill over and cover the retaining walls.

There are many statuary features, including Portuguese tiled garden seats or *alegretes*, as well as a folly said to come from Columbus' House in Funchal. Among the unusual species in the garden's many plant collections are several flowering trees, including arbutus, callistemon, and jacaranda. There is a Madeiran laurel, *Ocotea foetens*, and a large specimen of *Erythrina crista-galli* with its flame-red cockscomb-like flowers.

---

open: All year, Tue to Sun,
10am–12.30pm and 2–6.30pm;
closes 25 Dec, 1 Jan, Good Friday,
Easter Monday, 1 May

Further information from:
Mosteiro de São Martinho de
Tibães, Mire de Tibães, 4710 Braga
Tel: 053 62 26 70

Nearby sights of interest:
Museum of the monastery;
Bom Jesus do Monte (see p.108);
Jardim de Santa Barbara, Braga;
Jardim do Museu dos Biscainhos
(see p.108).

29 *Mosteiro de São Martinho de Tibães*

Location: 6km (3¾ miles) NW of Braga

In the 17th century prosperous Benedictine monks who had created an almost self-sufficient abbey economy at Tibães, replaced old buildings and styles and displayed their wealth in an explosion of Baroque splendour. Today the splendour has faded through a combination of neglect and changing times, but Tibães has survived and emerged from a disastrous period of private ownership and restoration work is in progress.

The neglect and decay has advantages for lovers of romantic landscapes. Moss-encrusted statuary, fountains, and wildflowers, such as daises growing out of cracks in paving, are among the evocative images at Tibães. Softened by moss and overgrown by vegetation the Baroque Calvary staircase offers a sense of peace and timelessness.

Casa de Mateus

Location: 3km (2 miles) E of Vila Real on the N322

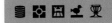

🌿 **open:** Daily, summer
9am–7pm and winter 10am–5pm

Further information from:
Fundação da Casa de Mateus,
5000 Vila Real
Tel: 059 32 31 21
Fax: 059 32 65 53

Nearby sights of interest:
Village of Sabrosa; Mondim de
Basto; Regua (capital of port wine
trade); Parque Natural de Alvão.

The first glimpse of the elaborately ornamented façade of Casa de Mateus, also known as Solar de Mateus, gives a taste of the garden delights to come. Reflected in the glassy, still waters of the Mirror Lake, the house shows off its origins, thought to be the work of the 18th-century Italian architect, Nicolau Nasoni.

The lake is framed at a lower level with hydrangeas and bergenias, and in autumn the colours of the trees are mirrored in its waters. The gardens descend a low hillside from the front of the buildings in a series of elaborate and intricate parterres. The first, on the same level as the buildings, has double box hedges, the inner lower than the outer. Each path or bed edge is marked by box clipped into a ball shape. An avenue of camellias lines the path at the back of the first parterre.

To reach the lower level the route takes you through a vast clipped tunnel of cypress. Inside the tunnel it is like being in a secret, child's world of gnarled bare tree limbs. Outside, the closely clipped tunnel is reminiscent of a magical monster gliding through the otherwise formal setting of the parterres. The last parterre of box, cut to few a centimetres in height, is set on light, beige gravel. On one side there is a stone *chafariz*, flanked by two upright, columnar cypresses. This parterre is separated from the others by a highly sculpted decorative wall of cypress, clipped into rounded sinuous shapes. The land falls away from the parterre terrace to a streamside walk and the open view is to the vineyards in the valley.

This lower parterre is backed by an impressive tunnel of clipped cypress.

open: Contact public relations department for opening times

Further information from:
Gabinete de Relações Públicas, Instituto Nacional de Administração, Palácio dos Marquês de Pombal, 2780 Oeiras
Tel: 01 441 32 31
Fax: 01 443 27 50

Nearby sights of interest:
Belém in Lisbon; beaches at Cascais.

31 *Palácio dos Marquês de Pombal*

Location: In Oeiras, 10km (6¼ miles) W of Lisbon off the N6

Built in the 18th century the palace dominates the site and is in use as the headquarters of the National Institute of Administration. The gardens, now open to the public on a regular basis, contain numerous pieces of important statuary and Portuguese tilework. The most impressive of these is on the tiled staircase and fountain leading from the upper to the lower terrace. The upper terrace is dominated by two huge specimens of *Araucaria bidwillii*.

A tour of the garden should include the 18th-century grotto complete with stairway and dripping water, known as the Cascade of the Poets. Also in the larger parkland are fish tanks, a picturesque dairy, and a dovecote. There are many ornamental garden areas within the smooth lawned expanses, as well as smaller pools and fountains on the upper terraces near the palace.

open: Daily, Apr to Sep 8am–9pm and Oct to Mar 8am–7pm

Further information from:
Palácio de Cristal do Porto, Rua D Manuel II, 4050 Porto
Tel: 02 609 31 92

Nearby sights of interest:
See opposite.

32 *Porto: Jardim do Palácio de Cristal*

Location: W of the city centre

The Jardim do Palácio de Cristal was named after a structure that existed on the site in 1865. The building of the palace was commissioned by the local horticultural society and was the work of British architect Thomas Dillens Jones. It was replaced in 1952 by a domed sports pavilion. The gardens are extensive and still hold features of the original garden which was designed by a German landscape architect, Emille David. Near the entrance is a formal garden with roses, fountains, and shrubs, bordered by two long shady avenues, one of planes and the other of limes.

Serpentine paths wind around a lake, complete with swans and other waterfowl, and from various points in the garden there are views across the River Douro. Woodland plantings following the slope of the land allow for prospects on different levels and lead to an avenue of horse chestnuts. Proud peacocks strut along the avenues, competing with waterbirds for attention.

The gardens are well used by children and adults for sport and school-oriented activities, but there are quiet areas to sit in and enjoy the views.

Closely clipped foliage plants make a tapestry of colour.

Porto: Quinta do Meio

Location: W of city centre on Rua de Entre Quintas

Quinta do Meio or Casa Tait is one of a number of *quintas* that belonged to the English families who ran commerce and the port wine industry. William Tait began the creation of this garden in 1881. It is situated on one of the sloping terraces overlooking the River Douro and the now mature gardens are a haven of peaceful birdsong in a busy city. Tait was in correspondence with Charles Darwin and knowledge about plants and birds passed between them. There is a *Liriodendron tulipifera* of great age, now named as a national monument. Among the groves of sassafras (*Sassafrass albidum*) and Judas trees (*Cercis siliquastrum*), where cockerels and hens strut freely, there is a collection of camellias, thought to hold rare Portuguese hybrids. Arum, clivia, and fatsia make bold clumps of foliage and in season their blooms offer ornament. On the terraces of the garden watsonias and *Iris kaempferi* grow well, while the stream and damper parts of the garden are home to bog plants, tree ferns, and mahonias.

open: All year, daily, 9am–12.30pm and 2–5.30pm; closes Public Holidays

Further information from:
Câmara Municípal do Porto, Divisão Municipal de Instalações Recreativas e Cultarais, Palácio de Cristal do Porto, Rua D Manuel II, 4050 Porto
Tel: 02 609 31 92

Nearby sights of interest:
Museu Romântico; Quinta da Macieirinha; Gabinete de Numismãtica (Coin Museum); Estaçao de Sâo Bento; Museu Soares dos Reis.

Palms and box hedges on the lower terrace.

34 *Porto: Parque de Serralves*

Location: In the suburb of Boavista to the W of the city centre, just off the Avenida da Boavista

open: 1 Apr to 31 Oct, Tue to Fri 2–8pm and Sat, Sun, and Public Holidays 10am–8pm; 1 Nov to 31 Mar, Tue to Fri 2–6pm and Sat, Sun, and Public Holidays 10am–6pm

open: As above

Further information from:
Fundação de Serralves, Rua de Serralves 977, 41500 Porto

Nearby sights of interest:
Exhibition of contemporary Portuguese art at Casa de Serralves; Museu de Arte Moderna.

Surrounding the clean modern lines of the 1930s pink façade of Casa de Serralves are 18ha (44½ acres) of the park, farm, and garden of Parque de Serralves.

The garden is the work of the French landscaper Jacques Gréber. Gréber was the main architect of the Paris Exhibition of 1937 and was responsible for many design projects in Europe and America.

The style of the garden is as clear-cut and sharply architectural as the house and although they are not exactly of the same school, they fit together

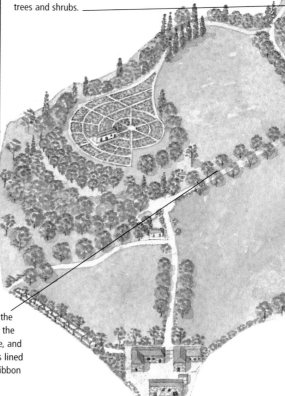

The Romantic Lake is surrounded by a luxuriant cover of trees and shrubs.

The route from the main garden to the Farm, Vegetable, and Herb Gardens is lined with a double ribbon of gazanias.

Avenues of sweet gum give way to tranquil open spaces.

The view from the fountain up to the Casa de Serralves takes in the formal elements of topiary and water channels.

The rose garden consists of numerous box-edged beds.

like hand and glove. As you enter the garden from the street and side of the house the first impressions are of shade from the avenue of trees, immediately followed by space as the formal terraces descend and rush forward like an aircraft taking off.

Close to the building are good examples of shaped topiary work in box, euonymus, and teucrium. Long avenues of mature horse chestnut run from the house lining the paths above the descending terraces. Leading away from the Casa de Serralves, at right angles to the horse chestnut avenues, are lofty canopies of sweet gum (*Liquidambar styraciflua*). In autumn the burnished foliage of the latter sets the site on fire. These avenues of mature, shade-giving trees and the sweeping lawns of the terraces accentuate the open aspect of the wide modern terraces in the central part of the garden.

To the left of the house is the Lateral Garden, a formal garden. Once more elaborate, it is now mainly lawn with neatly clipped box hedges and some topiary work.

Above and to the left of the central terraces are pergola-enclosed, shrubby areas where rhododendron and camellia bloom in winter and spring. As you move from shade into sun the shapes of plants and their shadows make interesting patterning on the sandy paths. In this area is the Sundial Garden filled with irises and other bulbous or tuberous plants. To the left of this is a rose garden backed by a colonnaded pergola holding climbing roses.

The uniform and regularly spaced shaped plants are part of the architecture of the garden.

To the right of the rose garden is a delightful restaurant and tea-house. Formerly the clubhouse for a sunken clay tennis court, it is lined with a pergola which "drips" white and blue rain from ancient wisterias.

The simple, elegant lawns are adorned by clean strong lines offered by long rectangular beds that follow the straight, geometric style of the dominating water feature. The planting in the beds within the lawns is startling in its simplicity and in its contrast to the pink façade of the house. The beds hold red-flowered salvias and cannas. Echoing the fountains, channels, and pools of Moorish gardens this water feature offers scope for meditation, as well as drama. The water rises from a pool near the top of the terrace system and is drawn away to what seems to be the edge of the garden in a narrow channel, with small falls as each level terrace is reached, and is collected in a pool with an elegant fountain playing. Behind it the garden falls away into a wooded area, with fine specimens of mature trees. The tree framework encloses the Romantic Lake, complete with island and waterfowl and their nest houses.

Once you leave the lake, terraces, and gardens behind, there is a wooded area to negotiate before you reach the open farmland of the Mata-Sete Farm and the Vegetable and Herb Garden. The roadway is lined with gazanias, in exuberant colours, making a continuous ribbon of colour at ground level alongside the road.

The elegant fountain at the far end of the water channels.

White and mauve wisterias entwined on a pergola provide a cascade of colour.

open: Daily except Tue and main Public Holidays, May to Oct 10am–6.30pm and Nov to Apr 10am–5pm
open: As above

Further information from:
Palácio Nacional de Queluz, Largo do Palácio, 2745 Queluz
Tel: 01 435 00 39

Nearby sights of interest:
Palácio Nacional de Queluz (interior); Estoril; Sintra.

35 *Jardim do Palácio Nacional de Queluz*

Location: In Queluz, 14km (8¾ miles) W of Lisbon

During the later years of the 18th century, the palace and its extensive grounds became a favourite summer home for the Portuguese royal family. The gardens were the work of the French architect Jean-Baptiste Robillion.

Entry to the garden is through the ornate and well-kept palace itself. If you tour the palace first, you will catch glimpses and views of the gardens at various levels. The

The Tile Canal was built in 1775. When the sluice gates were closed, the water level rose and boating took place.

Blue and white ceramic urns holding pelargoniums alternate with statuary in these formal gardens.

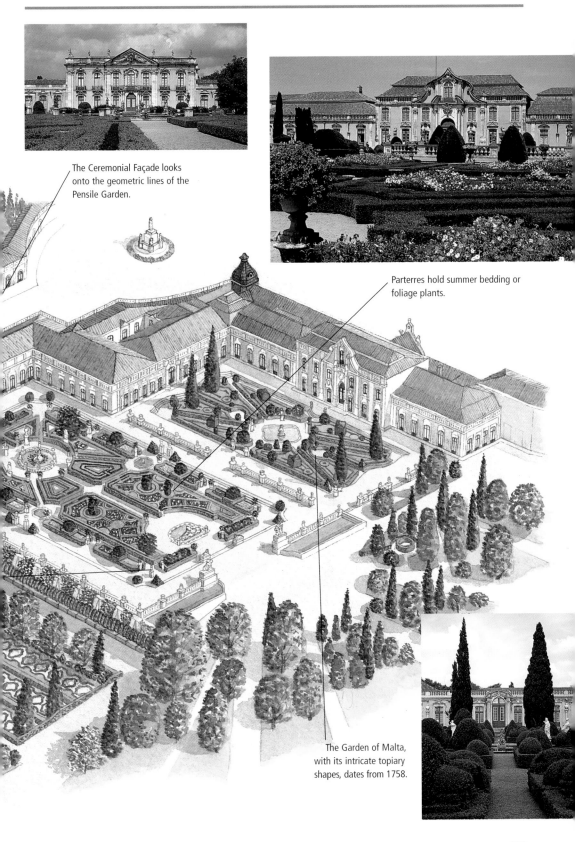

The Ceremonial Façade looks onto the geometric lines of the Pensile Garden.

Parterres hold summer bedding or foliage plants.

The Garden of Malta, with its intricate topiary shapes, dates from 1758.

Maritime scenes adorn the tiles on the Tile Canal interior, while pastoral scenes decorate the exterior tiles.

A lead statue depicting two boys and a dolphin in the central pool of the Garden of Malta.

two main gardens that connect the buildings are both formal, with geometric beds, statuary, and fountains, but each has its distinctive character.

The sunken New Garden or Garden of Malta was once a lake. Meticulously kept box hedging encloses lines of box ribbons, relieved by clusters of dome-shaped topiary at varying heights. The garden is surrounded by a five-tread stone stairway and the box has been planted to echo the curved indentation of the stairs.

Next to the Garden of Malta is a rectangular parterre garden, the Great Garden or Pensile (Hanging) Garden. It is built on the roof of the Palace's large water reservoir. Surrounded by stone balustrade-work its most imposing entrance is the Gateway of Fame, a statue of Pegasus bearing the heroic Fame. The Great Garden has numerous water tanks, pools, water statuary, and fountains. Each of the lakes has distinctive statuary and some have waterlilies adorning their surfaces. The Neptune Lake and the Lake of Amphitrite are at opposite ends of the garden, with the Monkey Lakes in between.

The two intricate parterre gardens on the upper terrace, with their statuary and water features, were much used by the court as outdoor reception rooms. Then, as now, the best views of the

parterre patterns were available from the balustraded raised promenades on all sides of the terrace. Colour impact between the hedges is made with dense plantings of purple-foliage iresine and blocks of silver-leaved plants.

In contrast to these two well-manicured formal gardens are the surrounding avenues in the parkland. Here paths radiate from central focal points and shade is offered from mature trees.

From Robillion's Lion Staircase it is a short walk to one of the garden's most beguiling features, the Tile Canal. Leisure was the principle *raison d'être* of the courtly activity in these gardens and nowhere is it easier to appreciate than in the Tile Canal. The stream of the River Jamor was led through the garden into this typically Portuguese tile-lined canal. Here the court and royal family sailed small boats on summer evenings and enjoyed music floating on the air from the Music Pavilion. Today the stream is no more than a trickle, but the tiles are in relatively good condition and evoke the scene of bygone days.

The most interesting pool outside the main gardens is the Medallion Lake. The former royal outdoor enjoyment in these gardens has been replaced by public appreciation of them with open-air concerts, ballet, and recitals in summer.

Stone benches set in box niches encircle the Fountain of the Medallions, which was designed by Robillion in 1764.

Typically Portuguese tilework decorates the façade of a raised wall planting of pelargoniums.

🖥 ⚙ 🏛 🍴 🦆 ⚘ 🏺

open: All year, daily, 10am
to 12 noon and 1.30–6.30pm

Further information from:
Caterina Vasconcellos e Sousa,
Casa de Santar, Santar, 3520 Nelas
Tel: 032 94 29 37
Fax: 032 94 29 33

Nearby sights of interest:
Mata Nacional do Buçaco
(see p.109); Coimbra; Viseu.

A topiarist's delight at Santar.

36 *Jardim da Casa de Santar*

Location: 10km (6¼ miles) S of Mangualde on the N254

This 18th-century-style garden at Casa de Santar is a topiary enthusiast's delight. The garden was restored in the early 20th century. Arranged on several terraced levels, all edged and divided by pathways, are a series of garden rooms enclosed by thick, manicured box hedges in a variety of heights.

The first level near the attractive façade of the house is a strictly patterned parterre with orbs, pyramids, and hedges in serried ranks. Circular and oval beds are planted with roses and there are a number of pools with fountains.

Fruit trees, artichokes, and other kitchen garden produce

fill the hedged areas below the main terrace. This terrace is separated from the lowest level by a dark and shady (on the inside) avenue of camellias. On the outside flowers and leaves glisten in the sunlight, and as the blooms fall they carpet the path, turning it pink, white, and red.

At the far end of the garden is a small lake. Fountains, pools, statuary, and a wall fountain or *chafariz* are among the architectural features.

🖥 ▨ 🏛 ⚘ ⚘ 🏺

open: Daily, summer
10am–6pm and winter 10am–5pm

Further information from:
Associação Amigos de Monserrate,
Rua Augusto dos Santos 2–4°,
1000 Lisbon
Tel: 01 352 82 68
or from Sintra Tourist Board
Tel: 01 923 11 57

Nearby sights of interest:
Jardim do Palácio Nacional de
Sintra (see p.138); Palácio de
Seteais (see p.138); Castelo da
Pena; Castelo dos Mouros; Sintra;
Colares (on the coast).

37 *Sintra: Parque de Monserrate*

Location: 3km (2 miles) W of Sintra on the N375

Monserrate is one of the most magical of Portuguese parks, probably because of its long connection with Anglo-Portuguese history and the evocative nature of its rise and fall.

The park occupies 50ha (124 acres) on the lower slopes of Sintra Mountain. The earliest building on the site is a chapel built in 1540 by a priest after his pilgrimage to Our Lady of Monserrate in Catalonia. It was in the 18th century that its Anglo-Portuguese history began, when it was rented to a British merchant Gerard de Visme. He built a splendid neo-Gothic palace which he let to William Beckford, who created the landscape garden. Among the stunning features are a cascade, a stone circle, and a fake cromlech. The beauty of Monserrate was legendary even then and in 1809 Byron wrote of a desolate house on the most beautiful site. But by 1856 the house and garden were in ruin and it was bought by the Englishman Sir Frances

Cook, whose love of the romantic style resulted in yet another change of appearance for the garden. He employed the landscape architect James Burt to design new plans for the park.

Restoration is on the agenda for romantic Monserrate.

Burt took advantage of the extraordinary beauty of the sloping site, as well as the variety of environments or microclimates that existed there, to create a series of gardens representing different areas of the world: Australia, Mexico, and Japan. One of the first grass lawns in Portugal was established here. Cook collected plants from all over the world, examples of which still survive in the park, including groves of camellia, tree ferns, palms, conifers, and ornamental trees such as the New Zealand Christmas tree (*Meterosideros excelsa*).

Changing family fortunes in the early part of the 20th century resulted in the sale of land and by 1947 it had been bought by a speculator who stripped the house of its valuable contents, then sold it to the State.

After years of neglect and romantic decay, almost as interesting as its romantic origins, Monserrate was included in the UNESCO World Heritage List in 1995 and, although restoration is on the agenda, the park's welfare is the concern of The Friends of Monserrate.

---

38 *Sintra: Parque da Pena*

Location: 4km (2½ miles) SW of the city centre

Parque da Pena is a 200ha (494 acre) area in the Sintra Mountains. It surrounds the Palácio da Pena and is part of the greater Parque Natural Sintra-Cascais. Ferdinand of Saxe-Coburg-Gotha, King-Consort of Portugal, built the Palácio da Pena in 1840. He commissioned the castle's architect, Baron de Eschweger, and the engineer Baron Kessler to draw up plans for the park, following the romantic trend of the 19th century. The existing natural features of the land were incorporated into a larger, "designed" landscape creating a naturalistic impression. Exotic features and settings were stage-managed, including the lake gardens complete with a medieval-style duck castle.

More than 2,000 species of plants, including cryptomeria from Japan, ferns from New Zealand, cedars from Lebanon, pine from Brazil, and conifers from North America, were imported and used to make the forests and woodland within the park. Camellias and roses are grown in a semi-formal garden area and all else is wayward and overgrown, but nevertheless evocative.

open: Daily except Mon; summer 10am–1pm and 2–6.30pm, winter 10am–1pm and 2–5pm; last entrance 30 minutes before closing

Further information from:
Palácio Nacional da Pena, Parque da Pena, Estrada da Pena, 2710 Sintra
Tel: 01 923 02 27
Fax: 01 923 43 75

Nearby sights of interest:
Jardim do Palácio Nacional de Sintra (see p.138); Palácio Nacional da Pena; Castelo dos Mouros; Parque de Monserrate (see opposite); Palácio de Seteais (see p.138).

Sintra: Palácio de Seteais

Location: 1.5km (1 mile) from the city centre on the road to Monserrate

open: By appointment but usually summer 9.30am–8.30pm and winter 9.30am–5.30pm

Further information from:
The Manager, Hotel Palácio de Seteais, Rua Barbosa du Bocage 10, 2710 Sintra
Tel: 01 923 32 00
Fax: 01 923 42 77

Nearby sights of interest:
Palácio Nacional da Pena; Castelo dos Mouros; Parque de Monserrate (see p.136); Jardim do Palácio Nacional de Sintra (see below).

Built as a palace at the beginning of the 19th century by the consul of Holland, a Dutch businessman, Daniel Gildemeester, the Palácio de Seteais is now a de luxe hotel.

The spacious front lawns and avenues of lime trees are a fitting setting for the buildings, which have matching façades and are linked by a triumphal arch built in 1802.

From the front of the arch you can see up to the Palácio da Pena and from behind it, there is an excellent view of the battlement parterre garden in the foreground and over the countryside to the sea. To one side of the palace is a box-edged parterre garden with cubes and spheres of shaped box, one of the oldest plantings in the grounds.

Sintra: Jardim do Palácio Nacional de Sintra

Location: In the city centre on the Praça de República

open: All year, daily except Wed, 10am–1pm and 2–5pm; last admission 30 minutes before closing time; free entry to gardens
open: As above; admission charge to courtyards inside palace

Further information from:
Palácio Nacional de Sintra, Largo Rainha Dona Amélia, 2710 Sintra
Tel: 01 923 00 85

Nearby sights of interest:
Palácio Nacional da Pena; Parque de Monserrate (see p.136); Palácio de Seteais (see above).

Tile seat and stone lion on the battlement gardens.

The Palácio Nacional de Sintra was built by João I between 1405 and 1433. There are Islamic-style courtyards and patios within the Palace, itself a formidable architectural treasure, and gardens on terraces outside on the battlements.

The interior patios feature many typical elements of Moorish style including water basins and channels, fruit trees, and walls decorated with colourful ceramic tiles.

The outer gardens can be enjoyed during the Palace opening times. Be prepared to climb from ground level on curving terraces and ledges to a courtyard high on the terraces, where there is a dramatic view across Sintra and the valley. On the way there are many attractive small garden areas. There are still some fruit trees and the vestiges of vegetable gardens, carrying forward the traditions of medieval times.

In the Jardim da Preta there is a relief painting in plaster depicting an African-American woman and a figure of a dandy standing by a low well and wash-house. Another exotic feature in this part of the garden is a tiled seat with a stone lion beside it. Box hedges contain small beds with roses and summer-flowering plants.

41 *Quinta das Torres*

Location: 25km (15½ miles) S of Lisbon

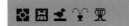

🏠 **open:** By appointment

Further information from:
The Manager, Quinta das Torres,
Vila Fresca de Azeitão, 2925
Azeitão

Nearby sights of interest:
Quinta da Bacalhoa (see p.107);
Setubal (old fishing port); Parque
Natural de Arrabida (on the
coastal road between Setubal
and Sesimbra).

The Quinta das Torres is a 16th-century manor house complete with pyramidal façade and Palladian *loggias* that open out into a courtyard, where a central fountain plays. Wisteria and other climbers drape themselves on the courtyard walls. The drive is flanked by olive plantations and citrus orchards.

The most evocative feature of the garden is the ornamental water tank. Rectangular in shape, its limpid green water reflects the dome, arches, and columns of a central pavilion. The manor is now a hotel and in summer it is possible to sit outside at the water's edge, enjoying the reflections.

There are beautifully planted containers, including citrus in *caisses de Versailles*, as well as secret private gardens, which can be visited with the owner's permission. Within these gardens *Chorisia speciosa* and jacaranda are among the mature specimen trees.

The dome, arches, and columns
of a central pavilion are reflected
in still waters.

Glossary

alcázar (Spanish) Moorish fortified palace

alegretes (Portuguese) raised built-in flowerbeds with seats

apeadero (Spanish) Andalucian covered walk-way entrance

azulejo (Spanish and Portuguese) glazed ceramic tile

belvedere (Italian) ornamental building in some commanding position from which a view may be admired

bodega (Spanish) cellar, wine warehouse

bosque (Spanish) forest

bosquet (French) formal grove, often with a decorative glade in which statues or other ornaments may be disposed

can (Spanish) Galician word for manor house

carmen (Spanish) Granadan villa with garden

cartuja (Spanish) Carthusian monastery

casa (Spanish) house

casita (Spanish) summer palace, but usually a small house or cottage

chafariz (Portuguese) public wall fountain, usually ornate

cigarral (Spanish) Toledan name for small country house, formerly lived in by minor clergy

estanque (Spanish) water tank, often ornamental in appearance

exedra (Greek) ornamental, open garden building which is often curved with a bench inside

glorieta (Spanish) arbour

hórreo (Spanish) Galician word for granary

huerta (Spanish) market garden, irrigated area

huerto (Spanish) kitchen garden, orchard

jardín (Spanish) garden

lago (Portuguese) lake

Lisboetas (Portuguese) citizen of Lisbon

Madrileño (Spanish) citizen of Madrid

mirador (Spanish) viewpoint

miradouro (Portuguese) viewpoint

Moçárabic (Portuguese) Moorish-Arabic style

mudéjar (Portuguese) Moorish-style decoration and architecture

mudéjar (Spanish and Portuguese) describes Muslim-Spaniards living under Christian rule, as well as a style of architecture created by Moorish craftsmen for their Christian rulers

palácio (Portuguese) country house or palace

palacio (Spanish) mansion or house of important and noble family

parque (Spanish) park

parterre (French) formal bedding with low hedges, often of box, disposed in a regular way and often incorporating topiary, urns, or other decorative devices. A *parterre de broderie* is a particular form in which the shapes are arranged in long flowing patterns

paseo (Spanish) promenade, also describes the typical Spanish evening walk

pazo (Spanish) Galician word for manor house

quinta (Portuguese) country estate or manor house

sardana (Spanish) Catalonian dance

sé (Portuguese) cathedral

sierra (Spanish) mountain range

solar (Portuguese) manor house

umbráculo (Spanish) wooden, slatted shadehouse

Biographies

de Villanueva, Juan (1771–1811) Spanish architect who studied in the Academy of Fine Arts of San Fernando, winning several prizes which helped him to be appointed draughtsman, under the orders of his brother, Diego, in the works of the Royal Palace. His first work for Carlos III was the construction of the *Casa de Infantes* in San Lorenzo.

Fontserè i Mestres, Josep Spanish architect and garden designer who built the grottoes and the lake of Parc Samà in 1881, and designed Parc de la Ciutadella in Barcelona. He inspired much of Antoni Gaudí's work.

Forestier, Jean Claude Nicolas (1861–1930) French garden designer who graduated from the École Polytechnique in 1880 and studied forestry in Nancy. He went on to become a landscape architect and worked in France, Spain, the USA, and Central and South America. He came to Spain in 1918 and designed several gardens, including the Montjuïc gardens in Barcelona. One of his most celebrated gardens is the Bagatelle, the rose garden in the Bois de Boulogne.

Gaudí, Antoni (1852–1926) A Catalan architect in the art nouveau style. In about 1900 he was commissioned by Eusebi Güell to design Parc Güell along the lines of the model of the English garden city.

Gréber, Jacques In 1937 he was chief architect supervising the work of 200 designers involved in the International Exposition of Arts and Technology in Paris. His clientele was varied and international. In Paris he was responsible for the design of the gardens of the Palace de Chaillot. His book *Jardins Modernes* (1937) expressed his classic principles while introducing his modernist tendencies.

Manrique, César A painter and sculptor who created a fascinating home on Lanzarote this century. An environmentalist who shaped his buildings to the extraordinary landscape of the island.

Nasoni, Nicolau An Italian landscape architect who arrived in Portugal in 1725 and introduced to the north of the country the fashion for Italian gardens, with terraces, statues, fountains, and belvederes. His aesthetic training showed itself in many of the designs for his Portuguese clientele.

Page, Russell (1906–85) English garden designer who practised in England, France, Italy, and Spain.

Rubió í Tudurí, Nicolau M (c1920) Pupil and associate of Forestier. Jardí de Santa Clotilde was begun in the 1920s when Rubió was a young man.

Sabatini, Francesco (1722–97) Spanish architect who studied in Rome and Naples, where he was appointed deputy director of the works on the palace of Carseta under his father-in-law. He was head architect to the King and of the Royal Palace, and he directed all the renovations and extensions to the royal buildings of Madrid when Spain was under the rule of Carlos III.

Index

Acknowledgements

I was welcomed into gardens and homes by many people in Spain and Portugal and received notes and suggestions from friends and colleagues. Thanks to them all and in particular to the following people for their time, expertise, and detective work: Barbara Abbs, Pepita Aris, Tom Bell, José Elías Bonnells, William and Rosemary Bowie, Jennie Bussey (Costa Blanca Gardeners' Circle), Mercedes Cervera, Roy Cheek, Catherine Dell, Caroline Erskine, Emma Gilbert, Heidi Gildemeister (for notes on Mallorcan gardens), Manuel Gómez Anuarbe (Association of Friends of Gardens of Spain), Paula Hall (Costa Blanca Gardeners' Circle), Vicky Hayward, Carol Kurrein, Michael Lloyd, Teresa Marques, Alan Mason and Marylyn Webb, Nigel McLeod and family, Joy Murray Barreto de Menezes, Paul Miles, Professor Josep Monserrat Martí (Botanic Institute, Barcelona), Rafael Muñoz-Bajo, Mary Rees, Sabina Rossini Oliva, Francisco Javier Silva Pando (Lourizán Forest Research Centre), Derek Toms (Secretary, Mediterranean Garden Society), Professor Benito Valdés (Seville University), Tony Venison, Dr Daphne Vince-Prue, Sally Williams (Garden Literature). Thanks also to Anne Dyball and Angela Clarke who travelled with me on occasions and shared some memorable garden visits, and to my parents for all their support at home. At Mitchell Beazley I would like to thank all those involved in producing the book, in particular Selina Mumford, Debbie Myatt, Jenny Faithfull, and Terry Hirst.

Barbara Segall, August 1998

Photographic acknowledgements

Front jacket: Explorer/Boutteville
Back jacket: Barbara Segall
Inside back flap: Derek St Romaine

All inside photographs have been supplied by Barbara Segall with the exception of the following:

Alfaqui/Alex-Cid Fuentes 63, /Javier Landa 39, /Manuel Molines 65, /Gerardo Ojeda 92; Heather Angel 13, 124; Roy Cheek 9 top, 57 top right, 58, 73, 78, 89, 90 bottom, 90 top, 91, 95, 96, 97, 98, 99, 100, 101, 120, 121, 123; Explorer/J Darche 133 top right; Eye Ubiquitous/David Forman 94, /Michael George 2–3, 36; Fototeca Internacional, Lda/Carmo Correia/Fototeca Viagens 134 top; Grassroots Productions 14 bottom, 20, 21 bottom left, 38; Robert Harding Picture Library/Nedra Westwater 76 top; Index 64; Tony Mott 21 top right, 22, 23 bottom, 41, 75 top; Clive Nichols Garden Pictures/Jardin Canario 93; Hugh Palmer 72, 79; Parcs i Jardins de Barcelona, Institut Municipal 29; Charles Quest-Ritson 47, 104 top; Scope/Jean-Luc Barde 86; Travel Ink/Simon Reddy 19 top; Francesco Venturi/KEA 42; Dr Daphne Vince-Pru 122